Make
Yourself
at Home

Make Yourself at Home

Discovering THE *Heart* OF THE *Church*

Kay Swatkowski

with

Raymond Swatkowski

Discovery House.
from Our Daily Bread Ministries

Make Yourself at Home: Discovering the Heart of the Church

Discovery House is affiliated with Our Daily Bread Ministries, Grand Rapids, Michigan.

Requests for permission to quote from this book should be directed to: Permissions Department, Discovery House, P.O. Box 3566, Grand Rapids, MI 49501, or contact us by e-mail at permissionsdept@dhp.org.

Library of Congress Cataloging-in-Publication Data

Names: Swatkowski, Kay, author.
Title: Make yourself at home : discovering the heart of the church / Kay Swatkowski, with Raymond Swatkowski.
Description: Grand Rapids : Discovery House, 2016. | Includes bibliographical references.
Identifiers: LCCN 2016023577 | ISBN 9781627074773
Subjects: LCSH: Hospitality—Religious aspects—Christianity. | Church. | Home—Religious aspects—Christianity.
Classification: LCC BV4647.H67 S93 2016 | DDC 241/.671—dc23
LC record available at https://lccn.loc.gov/2016023577

Printed in the United States of America
First printing in 2016

Lovingly dedicated to
LaVerne Margaret Swatkowski,
June 26, 1924–April 14, 2015.
She loved the church.

Contents

Acknowledgments

My husband and I love the church. By "church" I mean both the overall body of Christ (1 Corinthians 12:12) and the individual congregations of believers around the world who meet regularly for worship.

For forty-two years we have worked together in churches in Indiana, Illinois, Missouri, and France. Ray has crossed oceans to lead churches to greater health and effectiveness. As the years pass, our appreciation for the church has only grown. We believe the church is the greatest hope for the world.

Writing a book on relationships in the church has, at times, been overwhelming. Without the help and patience of key people, it would have remained a dream.

Our first thank-you goes to the loving men and women at New Haven Missionary Church in Indiana who mentored us during our college years. The memory of their passion for the church has never left us. These Christians modeled faithfulness and love, and taught us to pray.

We also thank our friends at Discovery House. Your support, kindness, expertise, and friendship made this book a reality. Miranda Gardner's enthusiasm and patience kept us going when we faced challenges. A very heartfelt thank you goes to our editor Paul Muckley. His expertise helped us work through many rough spots. We could never have finished without Paul's hard work and exceptional editing skills. Thanks to all who have spent hours helping us get this labor of love into print. What a pleasure to work with the entire Discovery House family.

Thanks to our children. Without your enthusiasm, support, and patience, we would never have finished. We appreciate your love and your being our greatest cheerleaders.

Thanks to our little grandchildren, Samantha, Madelyn, Holden, Aiden, and Noah, who too often heard the words "not now" or "later." Now that the book is complete, we promise many trips to the park and the ice cream shop. To our big kids, Nicole and Kevin, thanks for your help and constant reassurance: "Grandma and Grandpa, you can do this." We love you all.

Thanks to Gary and Marie Harrison and the board of Pinnacle Ministries, who have graciously allowed Ray time to work on this project. We are also grateful for the gift of spending time in churches around the world.

Though many stories in this book are composites of situations we have experienced over the years, with names omitted or changed, in some cases close friends *are* named, since their love for God and His people has touched our lives and deserves honor. Thank you to all who inspired these positive stories.

Finally, we are grateful to Jesus Christ, the head of the church, for preparing a loving family for everyone who believes.

But you are a chosen people, a royal priesthood, a holy nation, God's special possession, that you may declare the praises of him who called you out of darkness into his wonderful light.

1 Peter 2:9

Introduction

Never Neglect Your Heart

It was rush hour. Snowplows were busy clearing the streets, but not even a broom had touched the grocery store parking lot. I wrapped a blue scarf around my face, trudged through the slush, and grabbed a wet and icy cart. We just needed a few things for dinner.

Inside the store, as I rounded the end of the bread aisle and headed toward the dairy cooler, my heart began to pound so loudly I was convinced other shoppers could hear it. Panting, I hoisted a gallon of milk into the cart and then shuffled to the meat counter. Eager to get home, I even skipped the ice cream aisle.

It was bad enough putting my purchases on the checkout counter, but I realized with dismay that the most difficult part of this shopping trip still lay ahead—maneuvering the cart outside through frozen slush and snow. My imagination ran wild, and I began to wonder how long it would take a store employee to find my frozen body by the cart corral.

But I knew this feeling well—it had plagued me for nearly thirty years. Pushing a shopping cart, carrying a computer bag, breathing in cold or humid air, even at times just the process of eating could all trigger a rapid heart rate that left me weak and frustrated.

Doctors, never able to observe this recurrent condition, chalked it up to anxiety. Maybe, they suggested, it was related to an arthritic condition that flared from time to time.

After a while, I gave up searching for answers or asking for help. I just learned to live with the frequent frustration of having to collapse in a chair, lean on a wall, hug a tree, or clutch a shopping cart handle when my rebellious heart decided to sprint ahead of the rest of my body. I knew I had a problem; I just didn't want to think how serious it might be.

Then one day, my heart took off on a sprint of marathon length. After twenty-four hours of unrelenting tachycardia, I was unable to walk across the room. My exhausted heart wasn't pumping enough blood to my extremities, and I learned that when the heart is in trouble, nothing else works as it should.

I thought I was going to die.

Clearly, I survived that experience, but I learned a costly lesson: Never neglect your heart. If you do, expect to pay a high price.

The Heart of the Church

Today, some churches are paying a high price for neglecting their heart. They invest deeply in programs and spend hours brainstorming ways to stay afloat. But the cultivation of a thriving, deeply loving Christian community may take a back seat. I believe many churches are ignoring the symptoms of serious heart issues. They may sense the problem, but they don't want to consider how serious it is.

Over forty-plus years of ministry, my husband has planted and pastored churches in St. Louis, Missouri, and Menton,

France. Ray has worked with dozens of churches in the United States, and with groups of pastors in the Philippines and Japan, directly or indirectly impacting more than two hundred congregations. He has come to believe that the greatest challenges confronting churches today are relational.

When we as Christians don't connect meaningfully with other believers, we become discouraged. Our individual spiritual growth is impeded, and our churches' health suffers too. Whether we keep a cool distance or allow unresolved conflict at church, we will not be everything we can and should be. A light in our community will be snuffed out. Lack of love for one another dilutes our witness to the world.

The night before Jesus was crucified, He shared powerful words of instruction with His followers. After His death, resurrection, and ascension to heaven, Jesus would no longer be physically present with His followers. But He would still be visible to the world. How?

From that point on, the disciples' relationships with one another would change dramatically. Now, the world would see Jesus through the unity and love of one believer for another, the unity and love that reflected His love for them. This love—the heart of the church—witnesses to the reality of Christ's love.

> "A new commandment I give to you, that you love one another, even as I have loved you, that you also love one another. By this all men will know that you are My disciples, if you have love for one another."
>
> John 13:34–35 NASB

Jesus had come for this very reason. He appeared to unveil God's love in a way the world had never seen before. The love He commanded His followers to have for one another was revolutionary.

"One Another"

The gospel—the good news of God's love for humanity as shown through the work of Jesus Christ—provides the theological foundation of the church. The unselfish love of one believer for another shapes the emotional heart of the church. We need both.

Does your church suffer from any of these symptoms? Apathy? A lack of congregational commitment? Financial distress? Declining attendance? Volunteer burnout? Disgruntled leadership?

Ideas for a simple solution: Motivate people. Raise more money. Call a consultant. Start a new program or preach a sermon series.

However, if lack of love is the underlying cause of the trouble, none of these remedies will do. In fact, sometimes the treatment can aggravate a deadly condition and send the church into cardiac arrest. As with any health problem, an accurate diagnosis is crucial. So knowing what ails the church is the quickest path to finding a cure.

When my husband guides pastors and other church leaders through a process meant to revive their congregations, he often reads aloud a list of relational commands: "Love one another. Pray for one another. Serve one another. Accept one another."

Once, as he finished reading the list, someone excitedly asked, "Where does that come from?" Ray replied, "The Bible."

There are more than fifty "one another commands" in the New Testament. They give us a window into the kind of Christian community God has planned and desires for us. They offer us a plan to care for the heart of our churches, tools to self-diagnose and effectively correct our relational infirmities. By meditating on the "one another commands," we gain insight into the root of the struggles in many of our churches. We also find the cure.

Following these commands is not optional. If we neglect our heart, the cost will be much too high.

Heart and Home

When I was a little girl, we often took weekend drives in rural Ohio and West Virginia. On winding roads, we sped by small country homes. Some were perfectly maintained, with nicely groomed lawns and colorful flower beds. Others were broken down, with peeling paint and yards full of rusty car frames. Every house was quaint in its own way, but what attracted me most was the thought of the families behind those walls.

Did children live there? Did Mom laugh at their knock-knock jokes as she cooked at the stove? When Dad came home, did the children rush to greet him? Were there grandparents who played games and sang songs? I had an idealized view of home as a place of acceptance, belonging, and affection. That childhood view still tugs at my heart today.

Now imagine someone considering a church home. When they drive by our churches, are they wondering, "What programs do they have? What is their style of worship? Is their building new and up-to-date in decor?" Some people might be thinking that. But I imagine many will have questions similar to the ones I had as a child, sitting in the back of our family's Chevrolet: *Who are these people? If I visited this church, how would they treat me? Would the congregation accept me? Welcome me? Would fellow believers help me bear the struggles of life and encourage me when I am down? When I fail, will they love me, forgive me, and help me recover? Could we share a meal, a laugh, and life together? Can I trust them enough to confide my deepest sorrows? Would their love give me a glimpse of God? Would these Christians care for my heart? Would I truly belong and feel at home?*

Let's begin a journey, of understanding what it means for our churches to love one another, forgive one another, bear one another's burdens, encourage one another, and pray for one another. Let's see how the church should (and can) be a place of hope and healing, love and laughter, empathy and encouragement—a place where you can make yourself at home.

1

Members One of Another

Just Like Family

To embrace the gospel, then, is to enter into community. A person cannot have one without the other.

Robert J. Banks

Now you are the body of Christ, and each one of you is a part of it.

1 Corinthians 12:27

With an oversized black purse dangling from her forearm, Madame Hubert followed her husband from their second-floor apartment to the street below. With a fresh baguette tucked carefully under his arm, Monsieur Hubert guided his wife past bustling bakeries and flower vendors, and through noisy crowds at the Sunday vegetable market.

After walking three blocks, they took the bus from Beausoleil to Menton. The septuagenarians settled in to catch their breath on the fifteen-minute ride. The bus zipped along the snaking Rue de Gaulle under a morning sun suspended over the shimmering Mediterranean.

Madame and Monsieur were on their way to church.

In Menton, the Huberts walked a short distance down Rue Morgan, then turned right on Rue Albert. Only a couple more blocks and they arrived at their church home, L'Église Evangelique Baptiste.

Once inside, they turned their attention to breaking the fresh baguette and pouring out wine for the Lord's Supper. Soon they would share these elements with their beloved brothers and sisters, including Ray and me, who served as missionaries in this church.

Before our gathering in Menton, similar scenarios played out to the east. As Sunday morning broke over the South Pacific, island believers prepared their hearts to worship. Some walked to white frame buildings built on stilts. Others gathered in stone cathedrals. In remote areas, Christians strolled the sandy beaches to meet with other believers in the beauty of nature.

Small Japanese congregations met in homes or modest facilities. Chinese believers worshipped quietly so as to not attract attention. Some in Russia walked to onion-domed cathedrals where their families have worshipped for centuries. In Egypt, where many Christians face persecution, some met in white chapels with cupolas and crosses silhouetted against the blue Middle Eastern sky. Cement block or white frame churches, some built by missionaries, housed many congregations in African nations.

Farther west, as the sun rises over Brooklyn, Pastor Jean-Pierre unlocks the doors of Beraca, welcoming his Haitian congregation for heartfelt worship and teaching. In Pine Ridge, South Dakota, Gospel Fellowship Church embraces a handful of believers from the Lakota Tribe. Through several time zones, Americans gather in white-steepled chapels, aging brick structures, private homes, megachurch campuses, high school auditoriums, and a variety of rental facilities to pray, fellowship, and worship. Then, as twilight softly blankets Europe, Hawaiian believers begin assembling to adore Christ with their brothers and sisters.

For twenty-four hours, Christians in every corner of the world join in corporate worship and the sharing of the Lord's Supper. At any given moment, somewhere on the blue planet, a gathering of believers proclaims the love and power of Christ.

This is God's plan.

Regardless of where we live, or our social status, economic condition, political beliefs, skin color, gender, or ethnic background, we as Christians are one. We are part of a spiritual community that unites us in our love for Jesus Christ. The bridge that crosses continents and oceans and unites us with fellow believers in this:

> So we, though many, are one body in Christ, and individually members one of another.
>
> Romans 12:5 ESV

Why Community Is Important

The desire for community is a nearly universal human longing. Whether they admit it or not, every person has a need to connect with God and with others. As counselor and author John Townsend writes, "You have a God-shaped hole and a people shaped-hole."[1]

Our need is part of God's flawless design—just as varied organisms thrive in a coral reef, so we flourish in intentional, loving community.

Everywhere humans live, they gather in communities. It is as natural to us as breathing. Why? Community is necessary for the human race to survive the harsh realities of life. Living in a cooperative group allows for sharing the workload, pooling of resources, and caring for one another in tragedy and misfortune. Working together, life improves for everyone. Without community, humans suffer—and even die.

In 2004, Purdue University professor Daniel Aldrich visited areas of India devastated by a tsunami. In an interview, he described the important role community plays in helping people to survive disaster. Aldrich's research led him to believe that those who recovered the best from the tragedy were not the wealthy or powerful. Rather, he said, they were the ones "who knew lots of other people":

> Those individuals who had been more involved in local festivals, funerals, and weddings; those were individuals who were tied into the community. They knew who to go to. They knew how to find someone who could help them get aid.[2]

Aldrich learned that when neighbors had more intimate knowledge of one another's lives, they were better able to help in times of crisis. Commenting on the 1995 Kobe, Japan, earthquake, Aldrich said, "if you knew where your neighbors slept . . . you knew where to dig in the rubble to find them early enough in the process for them to survive."[3]

Who knows you so well that they could dig through the rubble of your house in the hour of your greatest need? We must have community to endure and to thrive.

What do you think of when you imagine a thriving community? A group of people who share an interest, a heritage, a religion, a cause, or a physical location? For many in the West today, community is less about survival and more about common values and mutual interests.

Some embrace other sports enthusiasts over games like football or hockey—with high fives and fist bumps, they find the camaraderie of sport uplifting and exciting. A violinist may join a fine arts community to build relationships with like-minded individuals. I know medical professionals who have a kinship through their specific cause, helping people get and stay well.

Most of our communities are limited in their scope and permanence, unable to address the deepest relational and spiritual needs of their members. Even people who never leave their hometown will find that other people do—because life changes. Groups that once met our need for belonging can pass away, but our need for community never changes. The longing to belong never fades.

Communities of the Heart

Humans are so desirous of community that we sometimes go to extraordinary lengths to create one—but whether that's the hippie culture of the 1960s and 70s or the gang culture of today's society, it just doesn't work. Even some religious communities, organized around a particular leader or set of rules, will fall short. The only true and lasting community is the one to which Jesus himself calls us.

Christian community is different. It is unique. The principles found in the Bible, when intentionally and faithfully applied, can shape a community that meets the deepest spiritual, relational, emotional, and often physical needs of believers.

What makes this connection among brothers and sisters in Christ so different and enduring?

True Christian community is constant and universal. It is always there. It is everywhere. While other things in life will change, the church as community is unchanging. Through each stage of life and difficulty we face, the church offers a place where we can grow and nurture the loving relationships people crave.

Since Christian community transcends geographical location and culture, the church offers us a place to call home wherever we may travel.

Stepping off a plane in Tokyo, Ray immediately felt lost. He did not understand a word of Japanese—either written or spoken. Fortunately, he was swept along with his fellow travelers toward customs and baggage, as he would never have found the way on his own.

Everything was different in Japan—the customs, the language, the food. There was fish with every meal, even breakfast. The Japanese dined on low tables, and their beds were mats on the floor. For three days, Ray felt confused and out of place, and wondering how he would survive his ten-day visit. Then came Sunday.

As Ray entered the Japanese church, he was graciously offered a pair of slippers. In most Asian countries, it is the custom to remove your shoes at the door. From the moment he arrived, Ray was cared for and accepted as a brother.

A man who spoke fluent English immediately introduced himself. Other believers approached Ray with smiles and welcomed him warmly. His translator was gracious and respectful while guiding Ray through the morning. He felt an immediate connection with each member of this Japanese congregation. They shared his love for the Savior, and they intentionally made him feel at home.

Today, Ray considers the Japanese as some of his dearest Christian friends. He has come to love the beauty of the Japanese way of life, which once seemed so foreign. That's because Christian community is constant and universal. It transcends geography and culture.

True Christian community is eternal, since it is based upon the eternal person of Jesus Christ. All communities have their ups and downs. Sometimes they grow, and at other times they decline—see, for example, Detroit, a community that boomed with the auto industry but recently fell into economic distress. And we only know of some historic communities because of written records or archaeological findings. Some communities just fade away and disappear.

But the Christian community is different. It persisted through all ages of history, and it will continue on into eternity. The people with whom we have fellowship today will be part of our lives forever. The relationships we form in the body of Christ today will never end.

The writer of Hebrews hinted at the eternality of our fellowship with other believers. Likening our Christian life to a race, he painted a picture of saints who have gone before us, circling our course and cheering us on. He not only encouraged the Hebrew believers to think of this "great cloud of witnesses," but to fix their eyes on Jesus—our link to those who have gone before.

> Therefore, since we are surrounded by such a great cloud of witnesses, let us throw off everything that hinders and the sin that so easily entangles. And let us run with perseverance the race marked out for us, fixing our eyes on Jesus, the pioneer and perfecter of faith.
>
> Hebrews 12:1–2

I look forward to meeting this great cloud of witnesses. According to Hebrews 11, David, Moses, Jacob, and Abraham will be part of this great crowd. Each of these saints shares our love for Jesus Christ. They are cheering us on. Someday, we and the believers with whom we now worship will join this "great cloud of witnesses." We will worship alongside them in God's eternal kingdom. We will enjoy an eternal Christian fellowship.

True Christian community is made up of believers who have been adopted into the family of God. Through our faith in Jesus Christ, we have become members of God's family: "So in Christ Jesus you are all children of God through faith" (Galatians 3:26). As members of the same household, we have obligations to one another: "While we have opportunity, let us do good to all people, and especially to those who are of the household of the faith" (Galatians 6:10 NASB).

Our place in God's home is guaranteed by our adoption—just as our grandson Noah came into his parents' home. On August 18, 2015, our daughter and son-in-law welcomed this three-month-old, with big blue eyes and silky dark hair, into their home. He is now surrounded by an extended family of loving grandparents, doting aunts and uncles, and silly cousins.

We fell in love with Noah the moment he entered Joy and Tim's home, and attached to him immediately. Within days I whispered to a friend, "We love him as much as if he was born into our family. There is absolutely no difference." From day one, Noah has been our little boy.

Within a few months, a judge finalized the adoption, lawyers were paid, and all papers were signed. At that time Noah became an official, permanent, legally irrevocable member of our family. Recently, Noah's older brother Aiden also joined the family. We celebrate that our family has grown through the adoption of these precious boys.

God has adopted His children just as surely as Joy and Tim have adopted Noah and Aiden. He has signed the papers. He has paid the price. We are part of His family, surrounded by brothers and sisters. It cannot be undone.

True Christian community is a place of love, belonging, and care, without discrimination. Everyone is welcome and everyone receives care. Consider the words of Helmut Koester, professor of

New Testament studies at Harvard Divinity School. In response to the question of why early Christianity survived, he said,

> . . . it gives even the lowliest slave personal dignity and status. Moreover, the commandment of love is decisive. That is, the care for each other becomes very important. People are taken out of isolation. If they are hungry, they know where to go. If they are sick, there is an elder who will lay on hands to them to heal them.[4]

The love and care of a Christian community makes a difference in the lives of individual believers. It brings comfort and support, assisting with our physical, emotional, and spiritual health, when we most need that.

Tucked away in the rolling hills of eastern Ohio, Finley Church was home to our brother-in-law's parents their entire married life. It has seen its members through hard economic times that included the closure of steel mills along the Ohio River, the shuttering of many local businesses, and rampant unemployment.

Through it all, the believers of Finley Church journeyed with John and Mary Ellen Ensell as they raised children and grandchildren. For weddings and baby showers, birthday parties or anniversary celebrations, these faithful Christian friends were always there. They sat with, prayed with, and walked with the family through illness, periods of transition, and grief and loss. The church was there when John and Mary Ellen each passed away.

For more than fifty years, the Ensell family made themselves at home in this church. The love and care of the Finley Church was a witness to God's love.

Sadly, many believers have never enjoyed this wonderful gift of the Christian life—the love and care of their spiritual family. They have never felt at home in the church. Have some of us perhaps lost sight of God's great plan?

Community Begins in the Old Testament . . . and Continues in the New

In the Genesis record of creation, Adam's communion with God was unbroken and uninhibited by sin. In spite of this vibrant friendship, God observed that it was not good for Adam to "be alone." So God created Eve to be Adam's helper, his companion, his wife (Genesis 2).

Several generations later, God's call to Abraham included the promise that he would be made into a great nation. God would bless Abraham, and through him, "all peoples on earth will be blessed" (Genesis 12:1–3).

Abraham's son, Isaac, blessed his son Jacob with these words: "May God Almighty bless you and make you fruitful and increase your numbers until you become a community of peoples" (Genesis 28:3). God did bless Jacob, ultimately changing his name to Israel, as forefather of a nation, a community, a people belonging to their Creator God. From that time forward, God referred to Israel as a community of people set apart to shine as a light to other nations.

God's plan for humanity didn't end with Israel. Through this favored nation came a Savior for everyone, who would create a spiritual community "from every nation, tribe, people and language" (Revelation 7:9).

Writing to "God's elect" (1 Peter 1:1), the apostle Peter reminded believers of their special relationship with each other: "But you are a chosen people, a royal priesthood, a holy nation, God's special possession, that you may declare the praises of him who called you out of darkness into his wonderful light" (1 Peter 2:9).

Our God is a relational God. In fact, community is modeled for us in the very personhood of the Trinity: God the Father, God the Son, and God the Holy Spirit, living together as one.

Much of the New Testament includes instruction on how we, as members of God's family, can live as one also. As chosen people, we are told to relate to one another in love. By caring for one another, believers shine God's light in the world. "By this everyone will know that you are my disciples, if you love one another" (John 13:35).

The Christian community is a God-ordained community. It is the best possible community. It should be a home filled with love.

Jesus Calls Us to Experience Spiritual Family

The church is like a body; it is made up of many parts, and each part is necessary (1 Corinthians 12:12–27). The church is a temple; we are the living stones that comprise the structure (1 Peter 2:4–5). The church is like a family; Jesus said so.

One time, Jesus's mother and brothers stood outside a home where He was teaching. They wanted to speak with Him. When told of their presence, Jesus asked, "Who is my mother, and who are my brothers?" Then, pointing to His disciples, He said, "Here are my mother and my brothers. For whoever does the will of my Father in heaven is my brother and sister and mother" (Matthew 12:48–50).

All those who follow Jesus are His family. And these brothers and sisters are to support each other. For some people, a commitment to Jesus would mean the loss of property and relationships, but Jesus made a significant promise to them: "Everyone who has left houses or brothers or sisters or father or mother or wife or children or fields for my sake will receive a hundred times as much and will inherit eternal life" (Matthew 19:29). Jesus acknowledged the importance of family and the pain of losing these relationships, indicating that a new family—a spiritual family—would be given to His followers.

This teaching was reinforced after Jesus's resurrection, when He told Mary Magdalene, "Do not hold on to me. . . . Go instead to *my brothers* and tell them, 'I am ascending to *my Father and your Father*, to my God and your God'" (John 20:17, emphasis added).

We who follow Christ become part of a new community, a family, a home.

Jesus Felt at Home in the Church

In Jesus's day, "going to church" meant a trip to the temple in Jerusalem or to a synagogue in another city. When Jesus was twelve years old, His parents took Him to the temple for the Passover celebration. At some point on the sixty-mile journey home to Nazareth, Mary realized Jesus was missing.

Where was He? In the temple. "Why were you searching for me?" the boy asked Mary and Joseph. "Didn't you know I had to be in my Father's house?" (Luke 2:49). It was only natural for Him to be there.

Early in Jesus's ministry, He traveled with His disciples to His own hometown of Nazareth. On the Sabbath, Jesus entered the synagogue and began teaching His own neighbors in a place where He had been taught as a child (Mark 6:1–6). He was acutely aware of the problems in the synagogues and the temple—after all, He was the one who cleared the temple of merchants who were exploiting the worshippers. Yet Jesus still valued spending time with people in that community setting. The temple, the synagogues, and small gatherings of believers became natural venues for His ministry.

Jesus validated community throughout His entire earthly ministry. His relationship with His disciples and the faithful people who followed their lead constituted the first "Christian" assemblies. They were loving and nurturing communities centered in their love and loyalty to their Master.

In His love for us, desiring to assemble a people that would praise His Father, Jesus created the church, a unique community of which He is the head. And He calls us to make ourselves at home in the midst of our spiritual siblings.

Make Yourself at Home

What exactly makes us feel at home in church? Programs? Not really. Style of worship? Probably not. It's not even tradition or a nice, well-maintained building.

Relationships—with our heavenly Father and with each other—make us feel like family. Warmth, care, concern, acceptance, and hospitality from our brothers and sisters in Christ make us feel at home in the church. Is your church a place where you feel welcomed? How about visitors to your church?

I have friends who are known for their hospitality. Jan and Jim were always scanning their church for someone needing a welcome. One Sunday, Jan introduced herself to a new couple and invited them over for dinner. After giving directions to her house, she and Jim hurried home to get dinner on the table.

Soon, the slam of a car door signaled their visitors' arrival. The host and hostess flung open the door to welcome their guests, and a beautiful golden retriever romped alongside the invitees. Jan and Jim reached down and patted the friendly creature on the head, greeting him as warmly as their guests. During dinner, the dog lay quietly in the dining room. At one point, Jan excused herself to fill a bowl with cold water for the panting pooch.

The afternoon slipped by with good food and friendly conversation. But when Jan and Jim's new friends rose to leave, the dog seemed uninterested in joining them. Jim coaxed the retriever, urging him to follow his masters to their car. Surprised, their visitors replied, "That's not our dog—we thought he was yours!"

The dog belonged to neither couple, yet made himself completely at home in our friends' presence. Without hesitation or question, Jan and Jim adopted the pooch as a guest and provided for his needs. Such generosity reflected the openness of their hearts.

What would change in your church if believers were more intentional about welcoming, showing hospitality and caring for one another with open hearts, open hands, and open doors? What if you deliberately extended a rich welcome to your brothers and sisters—or any visitors who happened to stop by? Everyone might feel more at home.

I want to make myself at home in church. Someone hand me an afghan and a comfy pair of slippers. Sit with me, sharing a cup of coffee and a story. Invite me into your life for laughter and love. I sincerely hope that you will feel at home too.

Together, let's see how the Bible's "one another commands" can help us develop and maintain the kind of warm, supportive church community we crave. Let's commit ourselves to living out these commands so the churches we attend can be places where members and visitors alike can make themselves at home.

BRING IT HOME

- Think of a time when you experienced a sense of "family" in your church community. What prompted that feeling? If you journal, write a descriptive paragraph or two as you process the importance of your church family.
- How many people do you know in your congregation? How often do you attend weddings, funerals, graduations, and other events that can strengthen your bonds in this community? Have you ever attended a small group? Is there a change in your thinking that needs to take place?

- Is there another believer with whom you are so familiar you could dig through the rubble of their home when disaster strikes? Does anyone know you that well?
- Pray for your local church, the body of Christ in your country, and your brothers and sisters in the persecuted church around the world.
- Meditate on the following Scriptures, asking God to give you a new love and appreciation for your spiritual family:

Stretching out his hand toward his disciples he said, "Here are my mother and my brothers! For whoever does the will of my Father in heaven is my brother and sister and mother."

Matthew 12:49–50 ESV

So then you are no longer strangers and aliens, but you are fellow citizens with the saints and members of the household of God.

Ephesians 2:19 ESV

As we have opportunity, let us do good to everyone, and especially to those who are of the household of faith.

Galatians 6:10 ESV

Do not rebuke an older man but encourage him as you would a father, younger men as brothers, older women as mothers, younger women as sisters, in all purity.

1 Timothy 5:1–2 ESV

2

Love One Another

So That All Can See

"This is My commandment, that you love one another, just as I have loved you."

John 15:12 NASB

When the world asks, "What is God like?" we should be able to say, "Look at the church." As the body of Christ, we are to be like Jesus; so that we too, reveal God to the rest of the world.

William R. L. Haley

She gathers books like some people gather friends. Her personal library of classics, dog-eared used volumes, and recent releases numbers over a thousand. During the first years of her Christian walk, Jennifer's intellectual bent drove her to hunger and thirst for truth, knowledge, and wisdom. She drank in the words of every sermon. She marinated in personal Bible study. Her devotion was slowly steeped in deep conversations with a few faithful friends.

In the study of God's Word, Jennifer's ravenous soul found nourishment. Her intellect was simultaneously challenged and satisfied. However, the idea of Christian fellowship escaped this scholarly, sometimes shy, new believer.

Real, live church people were secondary to the fascinating folks she found in her Bible and history books.

Jennifer's passion was to learn all she could about theology and living the Christian life. She was pleased to add new "friends" to her collection from time to time—a new commentary or a secondhand devotional with yellowing pages—but Jennifer was reluctant to get too close to other Christians.

One Sunday morning, she took her usual spot at the back of the sanctuary. From this safe place she could enjoy the music and relish the truths expounded by the pastor. She could also swiftly dodge hand-shakers and huggers at the end of the service.

Jennifer came to church for one reason and one reason only: to learn the Bible.

Studying the rows of heads lined up before her—some balding, some graying, some ponytailed—she quizzed the Lord about her fellow Christians. Wouldn't it be enough for her just to learn God's Word? Wasn't it good enough that she spent time with Jesus? What purpose could these people serve in her life? Sweeping her hand across the breadth of the room, she demanded: "Lord, what are they for?"

He whispered to her heart, "To love on."

That was not the answer she expected. It was not the answer she wanted.

It *was* the answer that forever changed her view of Christianity . . . and her life. As this dimension of the Christian journey dawned on her spirit, Jennifer's heart began to soften. Developing a relationship with believers wasn't about what she could obtain from them. It was about what she could offer. She began to embrace the command Jesus gave, just hours before His death: "Love one another, even as I have loved you" (John 13:34 NASB).

Observable Love

In *The Mark of the Christian,* a classic work on the Christian community, pastor and theologian Francis Schaeffer wrote of "observable love." He believed the most compelling argument for the truth of Christianity was "the observable love of true Christians for true Christians."[5]

Schaeffer's premise is in perfect harmony with Jesus's prayer for unity in John 17:20–21: "I pray also for those who will believe in me through [the disciples'] message, that all of them may be one, Father, just as you are in me and I am in you. May they also be in us *so that the world may believe that you have sent me*" (emphasis added).

This is what Jennifer ultimately learned. No longer did she perceive other Christians as unimportant—or worse, even a hindrance—to her learning and growing. Suddenly, the backs of the heads assembled before her came into focus as a missing piece of the puzzle. They represented an integral part of her own spiritual formation.

Jennifer was a member of the body of Christ. She was and is eternally bound to her fellow church members as spiritual siblings. The life of Christ that flowed through her flowed through them as well. Her spiritual growth hinged as much on loving and being loved as it did upon mastering eschatology. The credibility of her witness was linked to the authenticity of her love—her observable love—for all believers.

The love of Jesus is available for every man, woman, and child on earth. In the same way, our love for our Christian brothers and sisters must cross every geographical, generational, cultural, economic, racial, class, and educational boundary to spill over into the world. There can be no exceptions.

Jesus grants the world permission to judge the sincerity of our belief based upon the fulfillment of our calling to live in a loving community. "Your love for one another will prove to the world that you are my disciples" (John 13:35 NLT).

At times, we mistake our daily work for our highest calling. We live as if our personal to-do list of tasks and ministry responsibilities is uppermost in Jesus's mind. In our frenzy to get things done and create effective ministries, we neglect the heart of the matter. We overlook a key aspect of God's calling for our lives.

Loving others unconditionally should head our list of daily to-dos. Our Christian brothers and sisters—wherever they live, whatever their ethnicity, whatever their occupation or education—are here for loving on.

What Is Love?

Library and bookstore shelves sag under the weight of volumes addressing the subject of love. You can download enough digital books on love to use up the memory of your electronic devices. You could spend your entire life contemplating the mysteries of love.

We consult marriage experts, psychologists, celebrities, poets, and philosophers in hopes of uncovering the answer to this burning, age-old question: *What is love?*

The English word *love* covers a lot of ground. It is difficult for us today to make a clear verbal distinction between *loving* butter pecan ice cream and *loving* our spouse. The ancient Greeks were more fortunate—they had three words to define love: *eros* (romantic love), *philia* (brotherly love), and *agape* (sacrificial love).

Eros. This Greek word is not used in the New Testament. Yet the concept best describes most people's understanding of love. In conversations, I have noted that romantic attraction is usually what comes to mind when people discuss love. Our cultural preoccupation with eros love lays the groundwork for much disappointment, confusion, and pain in relationships.

Romantic love can be exciting, though it's often a fleeting emotion. It is not the kind of love Jesus commanded Christians to have for one another.

Philia. Having endured religious persecution in England, the seventeenth-century Quaker William Penn prayed his North American colony would be a place where everyone could worship freely. The Greek word *philia,* meaning "brotherly love," inspired him to choose the name Philadelphia for his key city. Ironically, Philadelphia became the capital of the American Revolution.

Philia and related words are used more than seventy times in the New Testament. While philia love is encouraged, it is never commanded. It doesn't need to be. Philia love is an emotional, responsive love. Affection, mutual respect, and camaraderie are the soil from which philia springs.

As the love of friendship, philia love is beautiful, inspiring, and touching. But it is still not the love Jesus commanded Christians to have for one another.

Agape. Eros and philia love feel familiar to us. We understand and enjoy romantic and brotherly love. But agape love? What did Jesus mean when He told us to "*Agape* one another just as I *agape* you"?

Eros and philia were the building blocks of the Greek and Roman conceptions of love. Then Jesus entered the scene to shake up the world's idea of love. He not only *introduced* agape love to the ancient world, He *demonstrated* it, showing us all a far better way.

Agape love is commanded love. Agape love is uniquely Christian love.

In his book *Your Father Loves You,* theologian J. I. Packer wrote, "The Greek word *agape* (love) seems to have been virtually a Christian invention—a new word for a new thing . . . it is almost non-existent before the New Testament."[6]

Unlike eros, this profound Christian love is not self-seeking or based on a romantic attraction. In fact, agape gives even when the love is not returned or the object of the love has lost its appeal. Agape love does not guarantee bliss, it promises meaningful relationships.

Agape love is not the emotion-based love of philia. It is an act of the will. The lover seeks the actual welfare—not just the camaraderie—of the loved. And it is characterized by acts of sacrificial service. Agape love consistently seeks the benefit of another person; it is always giving. Sound radical? It is.

Agape love may be hard to define, but we know it when we see it. And we see it in the sacrifice of Jesus Christ on the cross. He gave himself for us.

We also witness this extreme Christian love throughout church history, as believers have followed the example of Christ. Early Christians took seriously Christ's command to love one another. As the gospel writer Luke recorded in Acts 2:44–45, "All the believers were together and had everything in common. They sold property and possessions to give to anyone who had need." The church father Clement of Alexandria, who lived from about AD 150–215, wrote about the generosity of Christ followers, describing a man who "impoverished himself out of love, so that he is certain he may never overlook a brother in need."[7]

The early church understood the giving nature of agape love. It was not merely what the early believers did, it was who they were.

Agape Love Is a Consistent Biblical Theme

Walking with Jesus through the Gospels, from Matthew 1 to John 21, we hear the Savior repeat the same message, again and again: Love God. Love people. Love God. Love people.

Love is central to Christianity. Of all the definitions of love I have read, I find the Bible writer John's the most irresistible: "God is love "(1 John 4:16). Notice that God does not "do" love. God does not possess love. God *is* love. The character and nature of God is complete love. Every act, thought, word, creation, judgment, and emotion of God emanates from His loving nature.

Love is also an important aim for all believers: "The goal of our instruction is love from a pure heart" (1 Timothy 1:5 NASB). So the God of agape love has a mission for His people. He invites us to join Him in loving our fellow Christians: "And he has given us this command: Anyone who loves God must also love their brother and sister" (1 John 4:21).

Galatians 5:22–23 lists the "fruit of the Spirit," and love heads the list. God's Spirit within us produces agape love and enables us to fulfill Jesus's command to love one another. When we walk in the Spirit, God fills us with His love.

A chant sung in the Catholic church says it beautifully: "Wherever love is true, God is there."

Love as a Calling

My friend and counseling colleague Beverly often says, "The primary challenge of the Christian life is learning to love well." As we grow in faith, we recognize that love is a conscious choice to be unselfish. It is not a feeling but a decision to put other's needs before our own. C. S. Lewis hit the mark when he wrote "Love is not affectionate feeling, but a steady wish for the loved person's ultimate good as far as it can be obtained."[8]

Some say Christianity is for the weak, a crutch for vulnerable people who want to avoid the hardships of life. But wait a minute—name something harder than loving an enemy. Or caring for someone who is difficult, argumentative, draining, or dismissive? Holding our tongue, showing patience, forgiving "seventy times seven times" does not sound like a job for the weak. Learning to love well takes humility, commitment, courage, and perseverance. It is the hardest work we will do in this life. It is not for cowards.

Our usual list of spiritual disciplines consists of Bible reading, prayer, giving, serving, fasting, and solitude. Considering the repeated scriptural commands and the degree of self-control needed to love well, perhaps *loving one another* should be assigned the title of spiritual discipline . . . a discipline that should be practiced daily.

Loving Jesus and loving others are critical aspects of the calling of the Christian life. Loving well is our life vocation. The apostle Paul recognized that love should be a characteristic of our daily lives: "Walk in the way of love, just as Christ loved us and gave himself up for us as a fragrant offering and sacrifice to God" (Ephesians 5:2).

The Law or Love?

The Jews of Jesus's day numbered the laws of the Torah at 613. They designated some of the laws as "light" and others as "weighty." In Matthew 22:36–40, a Jewish legal expert tested Jesus by asking Him, "Teacher, which is the greatest commandment in the Law?"

Some in the audience may have guessed that He would say that circumcision was the greatest law. After all, that ritual symbolized the Jews' faithfulness to the God of Abraham. Others might have placed bets that keeping the Sabbath was the greatest commandment. It certainly was difficult to keep, but it made a statement of their holiness before their pagan neighbors. Or would Jesus mention laws about sacrifices? Any religious person understood that sacrifice was critical to temple worship. It identified the Jews as God's chosen people. The Jewish leadership was very proud of the way it followed those 613 rules.

So imagine the surprise—even alarm—on their faces when Jesus replied, "'Love the Lord your God with all your heart and with all your soul and with all your mind.' This is the first and greatest commandment. And the second is like it: 'Love your neighbor as yourself.' All the Law and the Prophets hang on these two commandments."

Jesus made it clear that love is not a side issue. Loving others is paramount to the spiritual life. If you don't love God and love people, your spiritual health is in grave danger. If you don't love people, the law is a moot point.

A young husband and father confronted a crisis in his marriage. Like many of the Jewish leaders of Jesus's day, he was hard-working and perfectionistic. Getting things done and doing them well was his top priority. But this approach occasionally made him insensitive and unaware of his wife and children's needs. There would be time for them later.

One day God got his attention, whispering that this attitude was sinful. The man wrestled with God, but God won. Productivity had first place in his life; his family had fallen to second. This realization broke his heart. Something had to change quickly.

He grabbed his Bible, opening it to 1 Corinthians 13, exactly the cure the apostle Paul would have prescribed. Meditating on the words of this well-known "love chapter," it seemed as if each phrase applied to his own life:

Love is patient
Love is kind
It does not envy
It does not boast
It is not proud
It is not rude
It is not self-seeking
It is not easily angered
It keeps no record of wrong

It rejoices with the truth
It always protects
It always trusts
It always hopes
It always perseveres
Love never fails

1 Corinthians 13 lays a great foundation for a home built on love. But we need to understand the context of these powerful verses: Paul was writing to a conflicted *church*, often in turmoil. The people were divisive, more committed to personalities than to Christ. They were taking each other to the secular court system. They tolerated immorality, which was destroying relationships. They were legalistic and judgmental. They acted selfishly, even while celebrating the Lord's Supper. They even misused the gifts God gave them for building up the body.

This was not a church you could comfortably call "home." These people had lost sight of the heart of the church, the love that permeated those early believers in Jerusalem. Paul told these Corinthians believers, "I will show you the most excellent way"—the way of agape love.

Loving well in our families is critical. Loving well in the church is a holy calling.

Loving with Sincerity

Love must be sincere.

Romans 12:9

I sometimes dream of building a log cabin in God's country— the woods and hills of West Virginia. Maybe we'd clear a plot of land near the old village of Sincerity. When asked, "Where y'all from?" I would adjust my straw hat and answer, "Why, we live in Sincerity!"

It seems this tiny town, not far from farmland once owned by my great-grandfather, has been abandoned. I can locate it on a West Virginia map, but so far, my Internet searches uncover no record of businesses or current residents. (If you call Sincerity your home, I sincerely apologize for overlooking you.)

Whatever happened to sincerity? Not just the town in West Virginia, but sincerity in relationships. It may be out there, but sometimes it seems hard to find.

Dictionaries dispute the origin of the word *sincere*. Some say it comes from two Latin words, *sine* (without) and *cero* (wax). This particular story paints a vivid picture.

Roman marble workers lived in fear of scuffing or breaking the precious material they used for sculpting. One slip of the chisel could spell disaster. So sly sculptors used wax to fill in cracks and chips, giving their artwork the appearance of perfection. Purchasers were happy until they placed their statues in the sunshine. When the heat melted the wax, flaws were revealed.

It is never good to make things look better than they actually are. We can be sure that the heat of life—the inevitable struggles and disappointments—will eventually reveal all of our flaws. Let's admit our own flaws, and accept the flaws of our brothers and sisters.

The apostle Paul told the believers in Rome, "Love must be sincere" (Romans 12:9). The New American Standard Bible uses the phrase *without hypocrisy*. When people tell me the reasons they have abandoned the church, I frequently hear this passionate justification: "All Christians are hypocrites." I've learned to resist my first inclination to protest and defend myself and my fellow believers.

I have come to realize the hypocrisy people speak of is not entirely about beliefs or behaviors. What they dislike is a lack of love and acceptance in the church. They see a double standard as believers often praise the love of God but don't extend that love to hurting people.

Many people making their way into church buildings on Sunday morning look like Christians, talk like Christians, sing like Christians. They speak of their love for God. But, when the heat is on, their wax melts and drips, revealing their chips and cracks. Their (or perhaps *our*) gossip, critical attitudes, rejection, and harsh judgment damage everyone's perception of Christianity. The world expects a community of love from the church.

This is particularly true of the young adult generation often referred to as the millennials. They are abandoning church at frightening rates. Over ten years, the Barna Group interviewed twenty-seven thousand members of this demographic. According to Barna's research, only 8 percent don't attend church because it seems "out of date." Rather, 87 percent of people in this age group believe the church is judgmental, 85 percent say the church is hypocritical, and 70 percent of young adults believe the church is insensitive.[9]

Allowing for the fact that some respondents may be expressing a disagreement with biblical standards of behavior, I think it's fair to say millennials are looking for a sincere, loving community . . . a place to make themselves at home.

Loving Above and Beyond

In biblical Thessalonica, believers were known for their love. Paul commended them for this, while at the same time challenging them to go above and beyond. "Now as to the love of the brethren, you have no need for anyone to write to you, for you yourselves are taught by God to love one another; for indeed you do practice it toward all the brethren who are in all Macedonia. But we urge you, brethren, to excel still more" (1 Thessalonians 4:9–10 NASB).

"Excel still more." The apostle encouraged them to excel in love: to go above and beyond in love. Give a little more effort. A little more sacrifice. A little more care. A little more support. A little more of their resources. A little more kindness. A little more prayer.

I love the title of W. H. Auden's poem, "The More Loving One." Much of the time, we are desperate to be loved. More often than not, we are disappointed and disillusioned because the people we count on fail us.

Sometimes we don't want to be "the more loving one" in our relationships—we'd much prefer to be "the more loved one." We want others to care and make the effort, to go above and beyond when we are hurting or in need. And we want them to do it *now.*

How different life would be if we chose to become the more loving ones in our marriages, homes, friendships, workplaces, neighborhoods, and churches. If our family members—including our spiritual family—were confident of our love, would they feel more at home?

If we invited them to sit and stay for a while, maybe they would respond, "Why yes, I'd love to!" Perhaps they would kick off their shoes, find a cozy spot, and share a cup of coffee. Maybe they would even feel safe enough to share their hearts.

A church that goes above and beyond in showing love creates a culture where believers are safe, cared for, and at home.

Love in Action

Loving above and beyond is a powerful thing, but it doesn't have to be overwhelming. When you see a need, take a step and meet it. Reach out to people who are lonely or hurting. Speak words of kindness and encouragement wherever you can. Trust God to guide you.

Here are a few examples of people who love in observable, "above and beyond" ways:

A Japanese pastor named Hikaru began the "Cancer Philosophy Café" in his church to meet the spiritual, emotional, and physical needs of cancer patients in his community.

Every Sunday morning, Matt and Chelsea make sure Sarah gets to church safe and sound. In her eighties, with numerous health issues, Sarah longs to be at church—and Matt and Chelsea make sure she is.

Alaina loves young people. In her job as a family ministries director, she plans Bible studies, mentors leaders, and initiates wild and crazy games that make kids laugh. More importantly, she lets them know they are loved. Her young friends never leave her presence without hearing the words, "Jesus loves you."

The food pantry at North Point Community Church serves three hundred families from its town. Dozens of volunteers spend one Monday a month setting out the food and interacting with people who need the basics of life.

Jan sits beside the bed of her cancer-stricken friend, Nancy. Years of friendship have knit their hearts together in love. Jan's final gift to her friend is to hold Nancy's hand as she prepares to leave her earthly home for her heavenly home.

Literally every day in the church, all around the world, Christians show an active love for each other. Some send cards. Others provide meals. Many give. Countless pray. When we care for one another's physical, emotional, and spiritual needs, we are engaging in the observable love Jesus commanded.

Transformed to Love

Sometimes, we just don't feel the love. We wish we could love with sincerity, and stir up warm feelings. It would be great to go above and beyond, but we just aren't motivated. Unfortunately, spontaneous, affectionate feelings just don't seem to appear when we need them most. What then?

There are two things to remember:

First, agape love is not always accompanied by feelings. Agape love is a strong and steady *commitment* to the welfare of another person or people. Agape requires devotion and sacrifice, a mental decision to care even when we lack warm, affectionate feelings. The Christian love we've been discussing is altruistic, completely for the benefit of the loved one.

Second, God can and will change our hearts. It is possible to cultivate positive, sincere, affectionate feelings for our brothers and sisters in Christ. The secret of this transformation is found in Romans 12:2: "Do not conform to the pattern of this world, but be transformed by the renewing of your mind." To change our hearts, we need to change our minds.

Since we live in the world, we sometimes think of fellow believers from the viewpoint of the world. Perhaps we think they should be more like us before we can love them. Maybe we're clinging to a catalog of past offenses. Sometimes we feel disappointment when members of our church family don't meet all our expectations. With thoughts like that, it is unlikely we will ever have loving emotions.

Spiritual transformation only occurs when we change what we believe. And we change what we believe by replacing bad thoughts with good thoughts—by reading and contemplating and seriously believing God's Word. When we do that, everything is transformed, even our relationships. We begin to see our brothers and sisters the way God does. If we have the mind of Christ, we cannot help but love God's children.

They don't have to be just like us. With God's help, we can forgive, restore, and reconcile. We don't have to dwell on our hurts; instead, we can follow Paul's instructions to the Philippians: "Brothers and sisters, whatever is true, whatever is noble, whatever is right, whatever is pure, whatever is lovely, whatever is admirable—if anything is excellent or praiseworthy—think about such things" (4:8). We can focus on the good in our fellow believers.

Do you believe your brothers and sisters are here for "loving on"? If so, what thoughts do you need to change?

A Houseful of Love

Our family pulls out all the stops on holidays. At Christmas, our decorating gets a little out of control, with lights everywhere—on the tree, on the stairway, on the mantle. Ray has an elaborate Christmas village that delights the little ones. A children's nativity set is placed under the tree. Last year, we even bought a hand soap dispenser that plays "Jingle Bells."

We dust off the high chair for the baby. We wrestle with the Pack 'n Play. As we prepare the menu, we keep in mind everyone's favorite dishes as well as special dietary needs. Attending to the little needs and preferences makes everyone feel at home.

On the big day, little ones squealed and shouted with excitement. It looked like Santa's workshop had exploded in our living room with the towers of gifts around the tree. Older cousins attempted to distract the youngsters with games and conversation. But it was futile.

On the patio, in the freezing cold, our son deep-fried a turkey. Other men in the family spent their time inside, watching him shiver while they sipped eggnog. Elsewhere in our overcrowded townhouse, women chattered away. Chaos reigned supreme. But I didn't care. How delightful it was to have all of our family together for Christmas.

In the midst of the pandemonium, our oldest grandchild, Nicole, stopped playing with her little cousins and stood up to announce, "This house is so full of love."

I retreated to our bedroom to compose myself. Nicole's words were the sweetest thing I had heard in a long time. She presented us with the greatest gift of the season.

It is also our prayer for the church.

BRINGING IT HOME

- The people in your church are there for loving on. Talk to your heavenly Father about your fellow Christians. Ask Him to help you love these people as He does.

- If observable love is a compelling argument for the Christian faith, how can you better reflect Christ's love to the world?

- What changes might you make daily to "live a life of love"?

- Is there a relationship with a brother or sister in Christ where you need to be "the more loving one"? Brainstorm ways you can go above and beyond in relationships at home and church. If you need direction, ask advice from a godly friend or church leader.

- Do you have any worldly attitudes or viewpoints about fellow Christians that you need to confess and change so that you will be free to love?

- Pray that your local church will become a house filled with God's love.
- Don't forget: "Wherever love is true, God is there."

3

Greet and Accept One Another

You're Welcome Here

Offer hospitality to one another.

1 Peter 4:9

*I*t has been twenty-five years since I have been greeted with a holy kiss.

As an introvert, I cringe during church services when a cheery extrovert announces, "Greet someone sitting next to you. Shake the hand of someone you have not met!" My first thought is that it would be more enjoyable to have a root canal.

Then I recall our French friend Madame Janvier.

A quarter-century ago, Ray and I planted a church along the Mediterranean, near the principality of Monaco, in view of the Italian border. The town of Menton was known as "the pearl of France." Somehow, God prompted the communist mayor to allow our Baptist church to rent an abandoned building that once housed a synagogue.

Though she had no official role, Madame Janvier looked a lot like the greeter in our church. The moment a member or visitor's toe crossed the threshold, she was there to welcome.

Madame Janvier especially loved children. Addressing me, she asked how the week had gone for *les enfants*. Everyone healthy? And their French? Did they make progress? What about the littlest one? She is so tiny. You must feed her more fresh fruits and vegetables. Then Madame turned her attention to our children, bending down to kiss each one's cheek.

To the French, these kisses are holy.

Each week, my husband tried to start the service promptly at 10:30 AM. It rarely worked. The minutes before the service were as significant to these French Christians as the service itself. The opportunity to greet one another with a kiss on the cheek ranked as highly with our French brothers and sisters as a sermon or a song would have. And all those *bisous à tous* (kisses to all) took a while. We Americans needed to learn to be more flexible with the starting time.

But adaptability here did not entirely solve the problem. Occasionally, we needed to pause the service for latecomers, who also received the traditional greeting. While Ray and I focused on time, our flock made sure each person felt welcomed and loved. This is a key aspect of hospitality. Our French friends understood that hospitality is more than a dinner party—it extends to how we receive and treat one another on every occasion. True welcome takes time.

And in time, Madame Janvier's true welcome even won over this introvert. My red-haired friend would reach out for a hug and place a kiss on my left cheek, another on my right, and one last kiss back on my left. The French reserve three kisses for family members, or so we were told. Madame Janvier's greeting made me, an outsider and foreigner, feel important, valued, and wanted. L'Église Evangelique Baptiste was family. I felt at home.

Back in the states now, when the Sunday morning host urges us to welcome our fellow Christians, I try to shake off my selfish attitude and look for someone I can help to feel valued and wanted. I hope to make others feel at home, just the way Madame Janvier did for me.

"Greet one another with a holy kiss" (Romans 16:16). The apostle Paul understood the importance of receiving one another with affection.

Kisses, Handshakes, Hugs . . . Whatever Is Appropriate

For the Jewish people of Paul's day, a kiss on the cheek implied affectionate friendship. The Greek word for kiss, *philema*, comes from the same root as *philia*—brotherly love. It is also the root of *philos*, which simply means "friend."

Some cultures kiss. Other cultures bow. For many years, Americans shook hands. Now, many of us fist-bump. Once in a while, we hug. The form of greeting doesn't matter. What matters is the value and respect we offer to our brothers and sisters in Christ. When we acknowledge a person upon his or her arrival, we communicate affection. We make them feel at home.

But how often do we greet others without being fully present? We are often distracted, thinking about other things or noticing someone across the room we would rather talk to.

When we stand or sit in such a way to be face-to-face with another person, we listen in a more active way. Our open body language, especially if we are relaxed and warm, conveys attentiveness and care. Eye contact and full attention fills other people's emotional tanks. How do we "greet one another with a holy kiss" in a culture that doesn't kiss? Focus on others and their needs. Give eye contact. Listen attentively. Be fully present.

Truly greet them. When someone meets me with a smile and eye contact, I immediately feel at home with them.

The Church Needs Hospitality

Church families need hospitality to flourish. The sharing of our gifts, time, and conversation draws us all closer.

I have mentioned that my husband works with struggling churches. Ray often asks them to complete a survey that reveals the greatest congregational need. Almost without exception, deeper relationships turn up as their greatest need. What nurtures relationship? Hospitality.

The members of our French congregation were scattered from the city of Nice to the Italian border. Those who had cars maneuvered along twenty miles of twisting highway and tunnels carved into the Maritime Alps. For our friends who used public transportation, getting to church could be difficult. Gathering with other members for hospitality during the week took effort.

Then someone suggested the rather American idea of a monthly potluck. This was something new for most of our French brothers and sisters. Bring a dish to share, we said, or stop at the *marche* on the way to church. Don't do anything fancy. Our goal was simply to spend time together.

The first week we had an overabundance of baguette. Another time, a man slapped an entire raw leg of lamb on the counter in the church kitchen. Our impromptu repasts may not have been four-star, but there was always baguette, cheese, salad with vinaigrette, yogurt, Orangina, chocolate . . . and laughter. Our humble potlucks began the process of bonding us as a family.

The word *hospitality* shares its origin with *hospital*. Hospitals care for the sick and support patients as they return to health. In the church, hospitality cares for people. True biblical hospitality can return a church to health.

When other believers throw open the door of their home to us, or a meal is carefully prepared and loving shared, or when we truly make time to interact with fellow church members or visitors, everyone feels valued. Hospitality is a gift that touches our souls. It brings healing.

Hospitality May Be Costly

Hospitality is not the same as entertaining. When we entertain, we try to amuse or impress. Entertainment directs the focus onto the host or hostess. They scurry around making sure everything is just right: Don't burn the meat! There are spots on these glasses. What will our guests think?

True hospitality, though, is warmly welcoming others with a desire to meet their needs. Hospitality focuses all attention on the needs of the guest. The host prioritizes the spending of time with the invitee. When we are hospitable, we give of ourselves.

The sisters Mary and Martha were dear friends of Jesus. He obviously loved them and enjoyed their company. In Luke 10:38–42, we read that when Jesus came to their village, they opened their home to Him in a beautiful act of hospitality.

But while Martha was preparing the meal, building a fire, setting the table, fetching the water, and wiping sweat off her brow, Mary simply sat at Jesus's feet. Martha was annoyed, about to cross the line between hospitality and entertaining. "Lord, don't you care that my sister has left me to do the work by myself?" she grumbled. "Tell her to help me!" Instead, Jesus reminded Martha that she was worried about too many things. "Mary has chosen what is better and it will not be taken from her." Spending time with Jesus is always the most important. It will never disappoint.

The early church understood hospitality. They needed to be together, as persecution made their relationships all the more precious. They gathered strength from sharing meals. They took in the homeless and fed the hungry. This hospitality wasn't sentimental or something you'd see on the cover of a supermarket magazine. It was personally costly and enabled the gospel to spread.

When the apostles traveled to share the good news of Jesus Christ, they were dependent upon the hospitality of believers in each city. God had planned for their generous support to advance His good news.

It is no surprise that the writer of Hebrews encouraged Christians to show hospitality to one another. "Do not forget to show hospitality to strangers, for by so doing some people have shown hospitality to angels without knowing it" (Hebrews 13:2). This was an honor and a spiritual privilege. It brought unexpected blessings. The writer of Hebrews did not want his readers to miss out on these moments.

Some of us say we would like to become more like the church in Acts. But would we really be willing to follow this example? "God's grace was so powerfully at work in them all that there were no needy persons among them. For from time to time those who owned land or houses sold them, brought the money from the sales and put it at the apostles' feet, and it was distributed to anyone who had need" (Acts 4:33–35).

Certainly, hospitality in the early church was costly. But that is not limited only to the early church.

Costly Hospitality in the Twentieth Century

The hum of clockworks, an hourly chime, or the clinking of fine tools was all you could hear at the Ten Boom watch shop in early 1940. The Ten Boom family—elderly father Casper and middle-aged sisters Corrie and Betsie—lived a quiet and uneventful life. That all changed in the month of May as the German blitzkrieg sliced its way through Holland and Nazi occupation disrupted everyday life in Amsterdam.

At any hour, day or night, German military trucks rumbled over the brick streets. Soldiers stormed houses and dragged horrified Jewish families into the streets, forcing them to climb into waiting trucks. In agony, the Ten Booms watched friends and neighbors being whisked away, never to return.

Corrie wrote about one of these experiences in her book, *The Hiding Place.*

> "Father! Those poor people!" I cried.
>
> "Those poor people," Father echoed. But to my surprise I saw that he was looking at the soldiers now forming into ranks to march away. "I pity the poor Germans, Corrie. They have touched the apple of God's eye."[10]

Christian beliefs and unselfish hearts set the stage for costly hospitality. The Ten Booms firmly believed that the Jewish people were the "apple of God's eye" (see Zechariah 2). When asked by the underground to hide Jewish families awaiting safe passage to the countryside, this Dutch family could not refuse.

The Ten Booms put their own lives at risk, building a false wall in Corrie's own bedroom to create a hiding place for their guests. The family shared the food they bought with their own limited ration coupons, along with cups, spoons, plates, blankets, pillows, books, pens, and scraps of paper. Betsie cooked the lodgers' food, washed their dishes, and did their laundry. Corrie became the underground contact and the lookout from Father Ten Boom's first-floor shop.

Many of the people who took shelter in the Ten Booms' home were strangers. Some were difficult and demanding. In the end, the family's sacrificial hospitality cost Casper and Betsie their lives. But their work on behalf of Dutch Jews saved eight hundred of God's chosen people.

No, hospitality is not entertaining. True hospitality costs.

Time and Hospitality

Christian hospitality continues to be costly and challenging today. We may not need to sell our possessions or open our homes to refugees. Not yet, at least. But hospitality still has a price tag. It costs us time and personal convenience.

Dorothy Bass, author of *Receiving the Day: Christian Practices for Opening the Gift of Time,* writes, "In an era when many of us feel that time is our scarcest resource, hospitality falters. If we are most comfortable when doing several things at once, does this not diminish our capacity to be still and to offer attention to a stranger or a friend?"[11]

Reviving the ancient tradition of hospitality will require a deliberate effort on the part of today's church—of you and me. In this era of individualism and technologies that tend to drive people into themselves, we need to be creative.

You may remember a time when church families shared meals. Aunt Martha brought her best apple pie and Miss Susan's potato salad was a hit. Children ran amok. Older people lingered over coffee and conversation. Recipes were shared. I miss those days! But this is a new day, and we must find new ways to share food, conversation, and times of prayer.

Old-time potlucks may not work in most places these days, but small groups are sharing dinners—it isn't as time consuming and still builds relationships. Picking up a prepared meal for a new mom may be a little inconvenient to us, but it certainly expresses love and care. We may have to carve time out of our schedule to visit an older person and share a cup of tea, but we will be glad we did. Opening our homes to aging parents who need companionship is a beautiful expression of hospitality.

Christian hospitality is simply love in action,[12] opening our hearts, homes, and pocketbooks to those who need us. It encourages relationships, furthers the gospel, and creates an environment where everyone can make themselves at home.

Accept One Another

> Accept one another, then, just as Christ accepted you, in order to bring praise to God.

> Romans 15:7

Recently, I had lunch with one of my dearest and oldest friends. Trish and her husband had three boys and one girl the same ages as our three girls and one boy. Our family attended the church that her husband pastored. She taught in the same Christian school as I had. We have so much in common and our conversation was easy and affirming. We laughed and reminisced.

All of us have an affinity with certain people. We share interests. We identify with one another's struggles. Our children may be of the same age, play on the same sports team, or attend the same school. Similar backgrounds, living situations, or educational experiences draw us together. We eat the same food, wear the same clothes, hold similar worldviews, and speak the same language. With some people, it is easy to relate. We have a high degree of comfort with our group and little annoyances are easily overlooked. We label ourselves as "accepting."

When the apostle Paul wrote to the church at Rome, encouraging them to "accept one another," many probably found that a bitter pill to swallow. Paul wasn't asking these believers to embrace their own social and religious circle. It was never that easy with the apostle Paul.

Believe it or not, he challenged the Roman Christians of Jewish background to accept Gentiles. Of all people! Non-kosher, uncircumcised, scorned, and rejected Gentiles.

Paul, that is a lot to ask—I mean, there are hundreds of years of bias and conflict to overcome. Steering clear of Gentiles has become part of Jewish life, doing it well a source of pride. How does one change his mind and behavior so quickly, especially about a group so detested? Maybe Paul had been out in the Mediterranean sun too long.

But the "Apostle to the Gentiles" makes a strong case for these Jewish believers accepting anyone who believed in Jesus as Savior. "Accept one another, then, just as Christ accepted you, in order to bring praise to God" (Romans 15:7). The Roman believers needed to see these Gentile believers for who they truly were—deeply loved and accepted children of God. The old divisions of Jew and Gentile were gone.

The Greek word translated *accept* in Romans 15 means "to receive kindly or hospitably." It suggests taking others—and I believe Paul was saying even those who are different—into our hearts. Accepting one another as Christ has accepted us requires us to welcome other believers with kindness, warmth, and hospitality.

Because He accepts, we accept. Because He welcomes, we welcome. Because He receives, we receive. When we accept one another in this way, we bring praise to God. We witness to His saving grace, extended to all who will come. We also satisfy a deep need of the human heart.

Differences exist. The variations of gender, nationality, race, language, culture, and age are gifts to enrich our lives. They're just differences, though we often make them divisions.

When, because of differences, we cannot accept one another in love, we divide the body of Christ. We may demand other Christians think and act the way we do. We might expect them to look the way we look. We pass judgment and withhold acceptance until they conform. Our differences become divisive.

We forget that, through faith in Jesus Christ, we are already one. The moment we choose to follow Christ, we each receive the same precious gifts: salvation, forgiveness of sin, the Holy Spirit. True believers are all clothed with the righteousness of Christ. Rejecting a fellow Christian over social status, nationality, or any other external factor is simply not an option for us.

Christianity is the most level playing field in the world. And it's a playing field where both the "home" and "visitor" teams should be welcome.

Accepting Differences

Joey hadn't been to many church picnics. He only came to this one because his sister was going to be baptized in the lake that afternoon. He was showing his love and support.

Unsure of what to do, he wandered through the crowd. Cheerful people balanced paper plates overflowing with hot dogs, potato salad, watermelon wedges, and brownies. Parents tried in vain to steer their children to waiting tables.

Feeling alone and out of place, Joey looked for a place to sit. Nearly every spot was already filled with people busy eating and engaging in conversation. He wanted a quieter spot.

Then he noticed a man sitting by himself. When Joey sauntered over and sat down, the man introduced himself. "Hi. I'm Jerry. What brings you here today?" Immediately, a friendship began.

Before long, Joey was openly sharing his thoughts with this soft-spoken man. He admitted he didn't attend church much. He felt uncomfortable there. You see, he gestured, people didn't much like his tattoos.

"Well," Jerry responded, "We are all the same. Some of us just have tattoos."

Jerry's kind response warmed Joey's heart. In time, he worked up the nerve to attend a church service. As soon as he arrived on Sunday morning, he looked for Jerry. Joey visited again, and again. The friendship between the two men grew. Most importantly, Joey accepted Christ.

Joey told the pastor that his spiritual journey had begun with a conversation at the church picnic. "Jerry accepted me," he said, "tattoos and all."

This wasn't the only person who felt safe and accepted in Jerry's presence. For many years, Jerry had been an usher. As he greeted people each Sunday, he formed friendships with many members of the congregation, including one timid woman who always peered through the sanctuary doors to spot him. Once she saw Jerry, she was able to walk inside as, without a fuss, he would quietly lead her to her seat. In spite of her anxieties, she always felt welcomed and accepted by Jerry. He put her at ease.

Over the years, hundreds of people have been greeted, welcomed, and accepted in just the same way. Jerry's unconditional love and gentle spirit have made many feel at home in this church community.

When we obey the one another commands to greet one another, welcome one another, accept one another, and show hospitality to one another, we invite people to make themselves at home in the church. The results are miraculous and heartwarming.

Acceptance in Action

Leviticus 19:32 encourages us to honor our older brothers and sisters: "Stand up in the presence of the aged, show respect for the elderly." Small gestures communicate respect to older people. Smile. Greet them by name. Hold the door as they enter the sanctuary. Ask them about their week. At church gatherings, insist they go first in line. Teach children to help them with their plates or chairs. Treat them as honored guests.

Take good care of the youngest family members too. As a little girl, Nancy was brought to church each Sunday morning. She remembers little of the Bible lessons, but can still recall the sweetness of cookies and Kool-Aid. Her Sunday school teacher made the classroom a kid-friendly space where Nancy felt loved and at home. Four decades later, Nancy was working in children's ministry with me. When I fussed and fretted over teacher training, curriculum, and schedules, my friend gently reminded me, "Don't forget the cookies and Kool-Aid!" The message was received loud and clear: "Don't forget to make the children feel loved."

Children had little value in the ancient world—perhaps that is why Jesus's disciples had such difficulty welcoming little ones. But how we welcome children matters to Jesus. "He took a little child whom he placed among them. Taking the child in his arms, he said to them, 'Whoever welcomes one of these little children in my name welcomes me'" (Mark 9:36–37).

And be sure your church is welcoming to those who've lived difficult lives. Harry had known better days. After a string of poor choices, he spent his nights on the streets or sleeping in shelters. Then, miraculously, Harry found Jesus and church. Most Sunday mornings, he arrived early. Planting himself in the middle of the foyer, he exuberantly greeted members with "Praise the Lord." Some worshippers walked in big circles around the unkempt man, pretending not to see him. Others were touched by his zeal and learned to love him. His sincere gratitude for his rescue from sin served as a reminder to the congregation of God's great mercy to them all.

Does your church welcome those who have suffered because of addictions, poor choices, neglect, poverty, or abusive relationships? Do you have a process for assisting them? How do you integrate brothers or sisters in recovery or in need of recovery into the life of your church?

Is your church user-friendly for people with disabilities? It takes more than wheelchair ramps, automatic doors, or handicapped parking to meet the needs of people who suffer from physical or developmental disabilities. Are greeters prepared to guide these individuals to classrooms or worship spaces prepared for their needs? Is the morning's message accessible for the hearing impaired? Is your congregation eager to love, serve, and fellowship with people enduring chronic physical or mental health issues?

When Jesus comes in all of His glory, there will be great honor for those who embraced and cared for hurting and lonely people in His name: "The King will say to those on his right, 'Come, you who are blessed by my Father; take your inheritance, the kingdom prepared for you since the creation of the world. For I was hungry and you gave me something to eat, I was thirsty and you gave me something to drink, I was a stranger and you invited me in, I needed clothes and you clothed me, I was sick and you looked after me, I was in prison and you came to visit me'" (Matthew 25:34–36).

Different Skin, Same Heart

If you ever have the feeling that you could and should have done better in this area, don't be too hard on yourself. You're in good company.

Even the apostle Peter struggled with the thought of taking the gospel to the Gentiles. He was Jewish, and he assumed that salvation was only for the Jews. God shattered Peter's misconceptions with a vision we read about in Acts 10. Soon it was crystal clear to the apostle: God accepts all people who have a heart for Him.

The very next day, Peter spoke to a group of Gentiles gathered at the home of a Roman centurion named Cornelius. "I now realize," Peter told them, "how true it is that God does not show favoritism but accepts from every nation the one who fears him and does what is right" (Acts 10:34–35).

The church is made up of men and women, boys and girls from every nation on earth. God shows no favoritism based on skin color, gender, social status, occupation . . . or number of tattoos. He welcomes into His family anyone who fears and follows Him. And so should we: "Accept one another, then, just as Christ accepted you, in order to bring praise to God" (Romans 15:7).

A young couple came to my office for counseling. A troubled marriage, a rebellious teenager, and a referral from their pastor led to a connection I might never have made otherwise. The husband's frustrations overflowed while the wife sat quietly with her head bowed. When I tried to draw her out, she whispered, "You can't help us. You don't understand our culture."

My first thought was, "She is right. I don't understand their culture. They need someone else."

But instead I choked out, "You may be right. But we have something in common." I pointed to the Bible. "Let's just start here." We talked for a moment about our mutual love for Christ. We had the same heart for God and our families.

Of course, we had differences, but as the hour passed, I heard this mother's heart-cry. I could relate to her fear and anxiety, and a little empathy and a few suggestions helped her relax. As the couple left, the wife turned to me and said, "I understand. Different skin, same heart."

We are part of God's family based on His love for us. That is a love all Christians share in. He accepts us on that basis, and we in turn should accept one another with open arms. Whether we're greeting one another, welcoming one another, or showing hospitality to one another, our job is to make fellow Christians feel at home, in our presence and in our churches.

The Real Purpose of the Church

Do you remember how I said I idealized the families living in those quaint frame houses I saw as a child from the backseat of my parents' car? I imagined homes where everyone loved, accepted, forgave, and enjoyed one another. Everyone belonged.

Maturity has dashed many of my childhood dreams. From personal and professional experience, I've learned that love, acceptance, and belonging don't come easily to a family. Disappointment and conflict litter many family's lives. Maturing together takes hard work. My childhood ideal can be realized, but not without a commitment to make our homes into loving, accepting places.

The same is true for the family of God. Many idealize the church as a place of immediate acceptance and belonging, as a family without problems. The truth is closer to this: we are a messy, sometimes challenging family comprised of adopted sons and daughters from all over the world, every walk of life, and all ages. Maturing as the family of God requires hard work, a commitment to building enduring relationships and creating an accepting environment where each person feels at home. This is the heart of the church.

Confronting our own selfishness is vitally important. In his book *Sacred Marriage,* Gary Thomas wrote, "I slowly began to understand that the real purpose of marriage may not be happiness as much as it is holiness."[13] That is also true of the church.

The real purpose of the church may not be our immediate, personal happiness, but the expression of God's love and acceptance to the world through our love and acceptance of one another. It is an environment where we must confront our own deep-seated selfishness and pride. By accepting those who are different from us, we grow and mature. We become more holy, and often more happy as well.

BRINGING IT HOME

- Greeting and acknowledging other believers honors them. What would you like to do differently in this area? Decide how you will greet other Christians.

- What thoughts do you have on Christian hospitality? Are you ever tempted to entertain rather than to show hospitality? Are you prepared for costly hospitality? What challenges do you face in extending hospitality?

- How could hospitality impact your church? How might offering hospitality change you?

- How do people know they are welcome in your church?

- What preparations has your church made to welcome and accept believers who are struggling financially, emotionally, physically or relationally?

- When have you seen differences turn divisive? What is the biblical view of differences? How can you be more accepting of brothers and sisters in Christ who come from different cultures or social classes?

4

Bear One Another's Burdens

Making Life Livable

Carry each other's burdens, and in this way you will fulfill the law of Christ.

Galatians 6:2 NIV

The frequent attempt to conceal mental pain increases the burden: it is easier to say "My tooth is aching" than to say "My heart is broken."

C. S. Lewis

Swaddled in a fluffy blanket, Megan's favorite teddy bear rested alone in a doll bed.

"Megan," her big brother, Dylan, asked, "what's wrong with Cupcake?"

Megan sighed. "He's sick."

"Why is he smiling then?"

Megan paused to think, before answering, "Because he is happy with the care I am giving him."

Even a five-year-old understands that when we care for others they feel loved. Whatever we can do to lessen an overwhelming burden brings relief to the brokenhearted and dismayed. And we who reach out find benefit, too. We get to share in Jesus's work and enjoy the blessings of partnership with Him.

Jesus came to lighten our burdens. He was, and still is, the ultimate burden-bearer. As oxen are yoked together to share a load, Jesus invites us to share our load with Him. Not only does He help us carry our load, He shoulders the larger part of it.

Jesus knew that many people carried crushing loads. The suffering of others pained Him, which may be why Jesus spoke His harshest words against the Pharisees. They were the architects of unnecessary, punishing burdens.

These self-proclaimed holy men not only multiplied the spiritual burdens of the Jewish people, they cruelly refused to help shoulder the load. "They tie up heavy burdens and lay them on men's shoulders, but they themselves are unwilling to move them with so much as a finger" (Matthew 23:4 NASB).

In contrast to the religious leaders, Jesus offers to walk alongside each of us. He shoulders the heaviness of our load. "Come to me all, all you who are weary and burdened, and I will give you rest. Take my yoke upon you and learn from me, for I am gentle and humble in heart, and you will find rest for your souls. For my yoke is easy and my burden is light" (Matthew 11:28–30).

In times of great stress and anxiety, whether I'm facing physical, family, or spiritual problems, I revisit this verse. I imagine Jesus stooping to get under the weight of my load. Suddenly, the burden of sorrow seems lighter. I am not alone. I get a much-needed breather. I can rest. A smile creeps across my face. I am happy with the care He gives me.

He bears our burdens.

Bear One Another's Burdens

On February 12, 1981, our third child was born. Weighing only six pounds, with dark brown hair and a bow shaped mouth, Julie stole our hearts immediately. As I held her for the first time, her breathing seemed raspy and labored. The nurse whisked her away, promising to bring her right back. It wasn't unusual, she reassured us. My husband also left, to give the news to Julie's big brother and sister.

An hour later, a nurse did return—but not with our little girl. She was awaiting an ambulance ride to the neonatal unit of St. Louis Children's Hospital, not far away. An x-ray had revealed fluid in her lungs. She was struggling to breathe. "We don't know what will happen," the nurse said, without empathy. Before I could even ask her what she meant, she pulled the curtain around the bed and marched off without a single word of comfort or reassurance.

I panicked. I was all alone. I had no one to turn to in order to process this terrifying situation. Of all the things I could imagine happening, this was the worst. I knew it was one burden in life that I definitely could not bear. What would we tell our two other little ones if we didn't come home with their baby sister? All I wanted was to hold our tiny girl.

The nurse had rushed away. Ray had not returned yet and had no idea of the crisis Julie faced. I felt abandoned and began to sob uncontrollably.

But then I sensed God's comforting presence. It was as if He was whispering to my breaking heart, "Don't be afraid. I am face-to-face with Julie."

The Lord had reminded me of this truth from a women's Bible study I had attended only the week before. We had learned that the Hebrew word for *presence* can carry the meaning of being face-to-face with another person.

In that moment, I knew that Julie was not alone. God was present. He was face-to-face with her. We had not been abandoned; Jesus would carry this burden.

When Ray returned, we watched as the medical staff prepared Julie for transport to the children's hospital. We called our church family to ask for prayer. Ray would follow in the car as I stayed in my own hospital room. He felt alone too. My heart ached for Ray as he left to be the one parent with Julie that night.

At the children's hospital, Julie was whisked to the neonatal floor. Ray hurried along beside her, only to discover that two deacons from our church had reached the floor before him. He was not alone.

Carrying a briefcase, Charlie Foster was ready to offer support and prayer. Norm Swanson, Ray's best friend, was there as well; with children the same age as ours, Norm's heart was breaking for our family in this frightening time.

At one point, Charlie opened his briefcase. Ray expected to see papers and pens but found it was filled with fruit and snacks to get the men through the night. Charlie had planned on staying as long as needed.

Norm stayed in touch with our church family, reminding them to pray as medical staff put IVs in Julie's tiny feet and performed a spinal tap.

The next morning, the pediatrician gave us a startling and welcome piece of news: all tests were negative. Julie's lungs were clear. She could soon join her brother and sister at home.

We were grateful for Julie's good health, thankful beyond words for God's presence. And we were moved to tears by the face-to-face presence of our Christian brothers and sisters, people who, for twenty-four hours, helped to carry our heavy burden.

Sharing the Load

Writing to Christians in Galatia, the area of modern-day Turkey, the apostle Paul gave a "one another command" in slightly different terms: "Carry each other's burdens, and in this way you will fulfill the law of Christ" (Galatians 6:2). The Greek word used here for *burden* indicates a heavy load. Picture a bricklayer trying to carry a pallet of bricks on his own—it's not possible. Such a load cannot be carried by one person. Without the help of someone else, the wall cannot be built.

In rural America during the eighteenth and nineteenth centuries, barn raisings were regular events. Barns were as essential to farmers as their own house. Cutting, preparing, and carrying the lumber to the worksite took days. Framing a wooden structure of such proportions loomed as an impossible project for just one family. Taking on the building alone would have been an unbearable burden.

So the community came together to help construct their neighbor's barn. Everyone played a part. Some people carried bricks for the foundation. Others hauled lumber and nails. Some provided support by steadying ladders.

And there was the emotional support of shared meals and fellowship. Neighbors bonded around the common mission, and cheered when the last nailed was hammered. Without the help of their friends and acquaintances, a farm family would have no shelter for their livestock or a place to store their grain.

Whenever any of its members needed the help, the entire community would pull together to raise a barn. This is an excellent picture of how the church should work.

It is impossible to build a healthy, caring church family without each member doing their part. Church leaders cannot carry this duty alone. Bearing one another's burdens—providing the care that people need to rebuild their broken lives—must be a community-wide effort.

We all share in each other's heartaches and concerns. Some of us can carry the load of physical needs. Others focus on prayer. Some can give of their resources. Still others "steady the ladder" as fellow believers reach for their goals. Everyone should cheer their brothers and sisters, and expect reciprocal encouragement in their own time of need.

Let's build a healthy church community, a place where brothers and sisters feel safe and cared for. Let's make our church a place where people can truly make themselves at home.

Everyday Burdens

The apostle John taught believers that their care and concern for one another was an indication of their love for God. "If anyone has material possessions and sees a brother or sister in need but has no pity on them, how can the love of God be in that person?" (1 John 3:17).

To be like Jesus, we must offer practical support to others. Our care and help can make difficult circumstances tolerable. At times, we may even be able to resolve people's problems—or they may be able to help with ours.

We each have daily burdens. Some are small and easily managed, while others are grave and incredibly painful. Often, pride isolates us from one another and we attempt to carry our unbearable loads alone. The fact is that we will never budge such a heavy weight, but we are determined to manage on our own. So life becomes messier and more awkward. Our vanity gets the best of us. Too embarrassed to ask for help, we muddle on.

Or we may see other people struggling under their load, just as we have struggled under our own. Perhaps we could come alongside, stoop under their burden, and shoulder the weight for a time. We would love to give them a breather—but will they let us? Whether we are in need of help or offering it, a humble and mutual submission allows us to fulfill Christ's law: "love your neighbor as yourself" (Matthew 19:19).

For more than twenty years, the ECR team (Extra Care Required) of Faith Church of Grayslake has provided financial and emotional support for members of their congregation and local community. Networking with other churches and social services, this ministry has provided assistance and loving care to hundreds of families.

Each week, Celebrate Recovery groups meet in over twenty thousand churches worldwide, bringing hope and healing to tens of thousands. With sound biblical teaching, loving accountability, meaningful fellowship, and consistent prayer, individuals are finding a way forward after grief, loss, abuse, or addiction. When people in recovery share their burdens, the load becomes lighter.

Dave Ramsey's Financial Peace curriculum is a regular educational opportunity found in thousands of churches. As Ray visits churches, he sees Financial Peace posters plastered everywhere. Using biblical financial principles, believers are getting out from under the burden of overwhelming debt. The freedom from financial worry enables families to plan for the future and share their resources with important ministries.

More than twelve thousand congregations worldwide have the one-on-one lay caring ministry known as Stephen's Ministry (Acts 6:1–5). Over seventy thousand lay people and pastors have been trained to provide personal, financial, emotional, spiritual, and practical care to church members in need. Creating a system of care within the church, believers serving in Stephen's Ministry are actively fulfilling the command of Galatians 6:2: "Carry each other's burdens, and in this way you will fulfill the law of Christ."

Every day, brothers and sisters in Christ are taking up one another's burdens. Sometimes, the load is lightened through formal ministries. More often than not, we shoulder those burdens as we offer kind words, acts of service, empathy, and prayer. By accepting the burdens of our Christian family, we make Christ's love visible to the world. We create an environment where even the hurting can make themselves at home.

Heavy Burdens

Mark's death at age thirty-six was a terrible shock to his wife, Katie, and their two children. Other family, friends, neighbors, coworkers, and fellow church members were overwhelmed with grief too. They packed the sanctuary the day of his funeral to say good-bye to this quiet, kind, caring, and loyal man.

For many years, Mark and Katie had attended a small group in their church. The couples learned together, prayed together, ate together, played together, and supported each other. After Mark's accident, this loving group immediately surrounded Katie and the kids with love and practical care.

Mark and Katie's families, of course, stepped in to help as well. But the small group quietly continued its care over time. Katie's friends understood that grief has no particular timetable, that she would need their support for months to come. The small group provided a housecleaning service every other week, and a few months after Mark's death, some men from the small group appeared at her door, carrying a small freezer. Within days, the group filled the freezer with casseroles and frozen food. Their generosity supported her as she returned to her previous work as a teacher. She felt her fellow believers' love, and it carried her through.

For many years this group had met to laugh, learn, love, and enjoy life together. They were family. Now, though no one could carry Katie's immeasurable grief, her Christian brothers and sisters could share the load. They gave her the time and space to recover, exemplifying the apostle Paul's words, "Be happy with those who are happy and weep with those who weep" (Romans 12:15 NLT).

Some of us are very good at providing care for people in the midst of grief or overwhelming loss. But often, smaller, more private burdens escape our notice. These seemingly less important burdens can weigh down a person's soul.

How can we care for each other's everyday burdens? There are thousands of ways. Share a cup of coffee with a believer enduring a loveless marriage—your simple presence may lighten the load of loneliness. Fill the dishwasher or fold a basket of laundry for an ailing friend—your efforts will make their recovery time less stressful. Pray with a brother or sister struggling with depression—your empathy sends a message of hope to their hurting hearts.

Small words, gestures, and expressions of support make a difference. As Henri Nouwen has written, "The friend who can be silent with us in a moment of despair or confusion, who can stay with us in an hour of grief and bereavement, who can tolerate not-knowing, not-curing, not-healing . . . that is the friend who cares.[14]

Our acts of kindness, whether large or small, create a church community where people feel loved and at home.

Bearing Long-Term Burdens

You can't rush burden bearing. There is no expiration date on the pain caused by life's complications. We may wish that our fellow Christians would get past their sorrow, grief, loss, financial need, chronic health problems, or marriage and family issues. Can't they just move on with life? Here is the reality of burden bearing: some people's needs are simply long-term and require patience and love on the part of others.

At a young age, Jordan was diagnosed with autism. His parents, George and Lori, were determined to give Jordan what he needed to thrive and enjoy life. Happily, they were not alone with this heavy load. Their brothers and sisters at Good News Church have surrounded Jordan and the entire family with love.

Sometimes, church members would give George and Lori a respite from Jordan's constant needs. Lori remembers one who took her son to a park for a one-on-one outing. A skilled photographer, Lori's friend posed Jordan in the park, hanging from monkey bars or swinging on a swing. She captured precious moments that revealed the wonder and joy of his unique personality. Her kindness not only gave Jordan a wonderful day, but brought delight to the heart of his parents.

Now, as an adult, Jordan resides in an assisted living facility. Wanting to nurture his independence, George and Lori sought out a church near Jordan's new home. They met with the pastor to explain Jordan's needs, and the pastor eagerly agreed to meet with Jordan weekly, helping him acclimate to the congregation. Imagine the joy of these parents when they heard their son was helping in the church's Awana kids program! An experience that once would have been impossible for this young man was now an important part of his life—thanks to the consistent coaching, mentoring, and love of this pastor and his congregation.

George and Lori got another big confirmation that this experiment with church was succeeding, when Jordan started calling it "my church" and the church of his parents "your church." Lori is certain that someday, these loving people who have helped carry the heavy load of Jordan's autism will hear the words, "Well done, good and faithful servant!" (Matthew 25:21).

Whether the long-term burden is disability, depression, chronic illness, past abuse, or a broken heart, those who are bearing heavy, painful burdens desperately need a place to feel at home.

Bearing the Burden of Sin

Bearing one another's everyday burdens or those that come from great loss is one thing. But carrying the weight of another person's sins? Many of us would say, "No, thanks."

When we look closely at Galatians 6:1–2, though, we realize that is exactly what the apostle Paul was commanding: "Brothers and sisters, if someone is caught in a sin, you who live by the Spirit should restore that person gently. But watch yourselves, or you also may be tempted. Carry each other's burdens, and in this way you will fulfill the law of Christ."

Of all the burdens we carry in life, none is more suffocating than the guilt and isolation brought on by our own sinfulness. Grief and shame may come in like a flood. Despair hangs over us like a threatening cloud. It is at these times that we need our brothers and sisters most. Who will walk with us on the path of repentance, helping us find the restoration we so desperately need?

Our Christian culture sends confusing messages about how to deal with sin in our ranks. Some call for "tough love," which would seem to be at odds with sacrificial service. I believe many have confused the idea of bearing burdens with enabling bad behavior. These two concepts could not be more different.

When we bear the burdens of a person who has fallen into sin, our priorities include counseling and other helpful resources, ongoing accountability, and the administering of grace. The goal is full restoration.

By contrast, when we enable we make excuses or gloss over sin, making it easier for a person to continue in their bad behavior. I think of enabling as "clearing the path" so the fallen person feels no need to repent or change.

Enabling is the easiest path, both for ourselves and the sinning person. Why? Because truth-telling always requires more courage than grace-giving. Restoration is a demanding and costly process. Repentance, confession, accountability, discipline, prayer, teaching, and the giving and receiving of truth and grace are activities that consume time and energy. It can be uncomfortable holding another person accountable, and we may prefer to avoid that. But when we do, the one needing restoration escapes the discomfort of confession, repentance, and accountability, as well as the joy of forgiveness and growth.

But when we do the right thing, the end result—restoration and full usefulness in the body of Christ—is worth the sacrifice.

Know that bearing with a brother or sister who has fallen into sin requires personal diligence and humility. "Brothers and sisters, if someone is caught in a sin, you who live by the Spirit should restore that person gently. But watch yourselves, or you also may be tempted" (Galatians 6:1). Facing our own weaknesses and limitations is important in this burden bearing process.

Burden bearing drains our emotional and spiritual tanks. When we care for a brother or sister in need, it is vital for us to maintain spiritual disciplines—the habits of daily Bible reading, prayer, and Christian fellowship—to replenish our own fragile souls. When we focus on the physical, emotional, and spiritual needs of hurting friends, we can easily set aside our own. But when we do that, we can quickly exhaust our own internal resources. We are in danger of burnout. We might even begin to resent the person in need.

Self-care is essential for burden bearers to remain strong. We can be of little help to others when we are living on the edge of exhaustion or teetering on a precipice of anger. Routinely ignoring our own very real needs limits our ability to bear one another's burdens. A good night's sleep, regular exercise, and healthy eating are basic things, but they offer a big pay-off for our health. Time with supportive friends or enjoying nature can recharge our batteries. These fundamentals of self-care allow us to be calm, steady, and compassionate burden bearers.

Jesus modeled appropriate self-care. Having taken on human flesh, He understood the need for food, rest, and relationships. The Gospels are filled with examples of Jesus getting away from the crowds. And He encouraged His disciples to take time to restore their souls, even when they were surrounded by a crush of needy people : "Because so many people were coming and going that they did not even have a chance to eat, he said to them, 'Come with me by yourselves to a quiet place and get some rest'" (Mark 6:31).

Understand that we are never solely responsible for another person's restoration. Being part of a larger community of restorers can lighten our load, since bearing with a fallen brother or sister requires a real sacrifice of time and energy. As we bear one another's burdens, we may need to lean on the wisdom and support of fellow burden bearers.

Our time spent alone with God and in the company of other believers, resting and renewing our souls, is as important to burden bearing as our time spent with the brother or sister in need.

As we bear another person's burden of sin, we must guard against crushing hope by laying on too much discipline. A sinning family member can be fully restored. The apostle Paul urged Corinthian believers to accept a brother who had received church discipline: "The punishment inflicted on him by the majority is sufficient. Now instead, you ought to forgive and comfort him, so that he will not be overwhelmed by excessive sorrow. I urge you, therefore, to reaffirm your love for him" (2 Corinthians 2:6–8).

As a counselor, I love the work of restoration. Week after week, struggling or fallen Christians enter my office, hungering for accountability and grace. One week the discouraged brother or sister takes tiny steps forward on the path. The next they can't even find the path. The way seems lonely and endless. Who will help them shoulder the weight of their guilt, shame, or the wreckage left behind by sin?

Every family is a little dysfunctional. But full-blown dysfunction occurs when we refuse to address a family member's problems. To minimize dysfunction in our church family, we must be willing to bear with those who have fallen.

When we hold one another accountable, we mark out a path to holiness that everyone can walk together. We create a culture where issues are not swept under the rug. The family is committed to health and integrity. Our church is transformed into a place where we can confidently make ourselves at home.

The Beauty of Full Restoration

Over time, tapestries fray. Threads become broken or snagged and work their way out of the picture. Those in the tapestry restoration business spend hours with delicate instruments, magnifying glasses, and bright lights, looking for the loose or missing threads. When a needy strand is located, the restorer gently pulls the thread back into place. Then it is secured alongside all the others, just where it belongs.

When we bear one another's burdens through the difficulties of life, we display the beauty of the church as it is meant to be. When one thread works loose, the entire body is affected. And when we engage in the art of spiritual restoration, we gently draw in those errant but still beautiful and colorful threads. We work with God in reweaving them into their place in the body. Then we are all complete and whole.

Like a family, we bear one another's burdens because of love. When necessary, we gently pull the missing thread back into its rightful place. We weave our brother or sister in a little closer, a little more tightly, hoping they won't come loose again.

Be Patient with One Another

To the church at Ephesus, the apostle Paul commanded patience: "Be completely humble and gentle; be patient bearing with one another in love" (Ephesians 4:2).

I remember reading an article that asked readers to consider some questions that grow out of that verse: Are you married? Do you have brothers or sisters? Do you have children, or still have your parents? Do you have an employer or coworkers? If you answer *yes* to any of these questions, someone has been patient with you. Someone has shown you forbearance.

We don't talk much about forbearance. Merriam-Webster defines it as "the quality of someone who is patient and able to deal with a difficult person or situation without becoming angry."[15] Forbearance is restraint. In legal terms, it is holding oneself back from exercising a right or exacting a debt.

The New Living Translation of Ephesians 4:2 can help us understand both patience and forbearance. "Always be humble and gentle. Be patient with each other, making allowance for each other's faults because of your love."

We all have annoying quirks and habits that can irritate other people. It is to our credit if we are able to overlook others' faults, making allowance for them and showing patience. "A person's wisdom yields patience; it is to one's glory to overlook an offense" (Proverbs 19:11).

But many of us have the kind of patience Margaret Thatcher, former British prime minister, described: "I am extraordinarily patient, provided I get my own way in the end."[16] We are impatient because we want our own way. We believe someone has infringed on our rights. We nitpick and retaliate. In these cases, we need to exercise forbearance in a major way—like the Old Testament character Joseph.

Joseph was his father's favorite son, the youngest of eleven (a twelfth would come later). His dad, Jacob, indulged Joseph, and the boy's prideful moments planted seeds of resentment in his older brothers' hearts. When Joseph shared a dream that hinted he would someday rule over his brothers, he lit a fuse of outright animosity.

Their hatred for Joseph exploded one day when Jacob sent him to check the brothers as they tended sheep. Jacob's older boys plotted first to kill Joseph, then changed their minds and sold him as a slave for twenty shekels of silver. Joseph ended up far from his home in Canaan.

Homesickness, slavery, betrayal, false accusations, and prison time marked Joseph's years in Egypt. But clinging to his faith in God, he survived it all. God placed Joseph in the pharaoh's court, where he was honored for his wisdom. He ultimately became a ruler in the Egyptian government, and prepared the country for a widespread famine that God told him was coming.

One day, Jacob's other sons arrived in Egypt, looking to buy food. Joseph recognized them immediately, though with the passage of more than a decade, they didn't realize who he was. At any time during their many interactions, Joseph could have exacted revenge on his brothers—from publicly berating them to putting them in prison and throwing away the key.

Instead, because his faith in God gave him love for his brothers, he exercised forbearance. Having identified himself, Joseph told his now terrified brothers, "Do not be distressed and do not be angry with yourselves for selling me here, because it was to save lives that God sent me ahead of you" (Genesis 45:5).

Joseph could have done the human thing. He could have lost patience with his brothers' requests. He could have paced the palace floor, ruminating on the abuse he had received at their hands, at the loss of his home and family. He could have returned evil for evil. No one would have blamed him. Instead, he restrained himself, showing patience and forbearance. He repaid evil with good.

I've never been thrown in a pit. Have you? More likely, our concerns are mundane, the everyday irritations that just get under our skin. A church leader overlooks us in a ministry opportunity. A fellow church member doesn't return our phone call. A brother or sister holds a different opinion during a church crisis.

Forbearance means we patiently bear with another person's idiosyncrasies or differing opinions. We restrain from impatient looks and harsh comments, and certainly from gossip. Remembering how we would like to be treated helps us bear patiently with one another. "Treat others the same way you want them to treat you" (Luke 6:31 NASB).

A Caring Community

The most caring community is the Christian community.

We are surrounded by communities—groups of people who gather together because of a shared heritage or common interest. Do you love gardening? Do an Internet search: you will surely find a group of garden lovers close by. What about sports? Do you belong to a soccer club or a hockey team? These too are an example of the wide array of communities open to everyone. Stamp collectors, food enthusiasts, poets, writers, artists, musicians—all have communities to which they belong.

Will these groups support and care for you? To a degree. Will they be your family? Perhaps. Can you make yourself at home with them long term? Probably not.

Will your garden club friends stoop under the weight of your overwhelming burdens? Some members might try to be of help. But that is not the purpose of a garden club.

Will the members of the soccer team walk alongside you as you are restored from sin? Chances are they are ill-equipped to provide that kind of care.

What other community is willing to dig through our rubble and pull us out when our world falls apart? What other community is commanded to provide long-term care for vulnerable and broken members by being the hands and feet of Jesus? What other community carries the expectation of being tender and patient and making allowances for minor faults? What other community bears our burdens in a way that reminds us that Jesus has borne all of our sorrows and knows all of our cares?

The Christian family should be the most caring family of all. In honesty, we all have a long way to go. Let's commit ourselves to bearing one another's burdens and creating an environment where we are happy with the care and love we receive.

"Bear one another's burdens and so fulfill the law of Christ."

BRINGING IT HOME

- Who helps you when your burdens seem too heavy to bear? What issue is currently weighing you down? Have you reached out for help?
- What is your attitude toward those recovering from trauma or dealing with the consequences of their own sins? How can you help to bear their burdens and show the love of Christ?
- Think of someone in your congregation who could use some extra support. What can you do to lighten the load? (Remember, you don't have to carry their entire burden.)

- How can you encourage a brother or sister in need of restoration? Don't forget: only Jesus can carry our burden of sin. "He Himself bore our sins in His body on the cross, so that we might die to sin and live to righteousness; for by His wounds you were healed" (1 Peter 2:24 NASB). How can you point people to the "sin bearer" Jesus so they can be healed?

- What situations trigger your impatience? Annoyance? Wanting your own way? Sense of unfairness? Talk to God about the source of your impatience. Meditate on His long-suffering nature. "But You, O Lord, are a God merciful and gracious, slow to anger and abundant in lovingkindness and truth" (Psalm 86:15 NASB).

5

Encourage, Build Up, Be Kind to, and Forgive One Another

The Quiet Work of the Church

> Therefore encourage one another and build one another up, just as you are doing.
>
> 1 Thessalonians 5:11 ESV

> Be kind and compassionate to one another, forgiving each other, just as in Christ God forgave you.
>
> Ephesians 4:32

The Washington DC Rock 'n' Roll Marathon takes runners past some of the United States' most historic monuments. Bands and cheering fans add to the thrill of running through the nation's capital.

In the 2013 race, as competitor Michael Stefanon approached the final stretch, he noticed a runner in front of him slowing down. The forty-four-year-old realized he could easily pass the younger man, but as the distance between them narrowed, Stefanon saw the other runner stagger. When thirty-two-year-old Ryan Gregg stiffened and fell backwards, Stefanon reached out to catch him, wrapping his arms around the exhausted racer.

Gregg's two young sons got to see their father finish the final fifteen yards of the race, helped in a big way by another runner who came alongside at the right moment.

The apostle Paul, who wrote of sporting events including races, would likely have approved. When he told Christians in Thessalonica, "encourage one another and build one another up, just as you are doing" (1 Thessalonians 5:11), the word he used for *encourage* can also be translated "come alongside." In Greek, it is the same root word from which we get *Parakletos*—the Paraclete—the name of the Holy Spirit used in the gospel of John.

Paul understood that we as Christians will sometimes lose strength and falter as we run the race of faith. He had faced discouragement himself, and needed others to come alongside him. Paul wanted both to encourage others and to receive encouragement: "I long to see you so that I may impart to you some spiritual gift to make you strong—that is, that you and I may be mutually encouraged by each other's faith" (Romans 1:11–12).

Though the Holy Spirit is the ultimate encourager in Christians' lives, we are all called to come alongside and strengthen our brothers and sisters as well. Our words of encouragement can infuse others with the strength to go on. When we mutually encourage one another's faith, we foster feelings of appreciation and affection and an environment where we can make ourselves at home.

Encourage: To Put Courage In

Author and psychologist Henry Cloud describes encouragement this way: "*Encourage* literally came from 'in courage.' The courage is put 'into' you from outside. Our character and abilities grow through internalizing from others what we do not possess in ourselves."[17]

In the spring of 1995, my parents lived in beautiful eastern Tennessee, about a thirteen-hour drive from our home. Both in their mid-sixties, they were going through a difficult time. Mom was recovering from surgery. My father was in a constant state of panic over her health. Fearful that she would die, he often phoned one or the other of his daughters to fret.

The truth was that *he* was the one who was dying. When we arrived in Tennessee the week before Easter, we expected to help my mother as she continued her recovery. Instead, we found my father had been admitted to the hospital with end-stage liver cancer. We all knew he had not been feeling well. But mother's illness had overshadowed his.

When I first stepped into Dad's hospital room, I knew he was dying. But my mother didn't seem to understand. His condition was more than she could absorb at that time as she continued to heal from her own medical procedures.

My father's misery and confusion were almost unbearable to me. After only one day of coaxing him to drink a little water or eat a bite of potato or say a few words, I was exhausted and distraught. I walked out of the room in tears. "I can't do this," I cried to Ray. "I can't go back in there. This is too sad."

"Oh, yes you can," Ray quickly responded. "You have to. Your mother isn't able right now. Your dad needs you. You can do this. You *are* going to do this."

I was staggering on the marathon of my father's illness. Ray reached out and caught me. His words spurred me on, infusing me with courage that I could not muster on my own. I couldn't give my dad a cure. I couldn't take away his pain. My efforts were small and seemingly insignificant. But he needed me.

It was Dad's final evening on earth. He was restless in his sleep, but awoke for a moment and agreed to a bit of pumpkin pie. He said it was good.

Sitting alone in his quiet room, I was filled with anxiety. To calm us both, I read Psalm 23 aloud. Dad occasionally seemed to hear and understand. Those comforting words were my good-bye to him. A few hours later he went into respiratory arrest, and passed away on the morning of Good Friday.

I am thankful now that I didn't withdraw during my father's last days. I am so grateful for Ray's encouragement. It is a picture of what our extended Christian family can and should be.

We often find ourselves in situations that require more strength than we have. When our brothers and sisters come alongside with encouraging words and loving support, our courage is renewed. We can continue to run the marathon of life.

The race the Thessalonians found themselves in was not a sprint. Paul was writing about troublesome times coming upon believers. It wasn't going to be easy to make it to the finish line. They would need the encouragement of fellow Christians to remain faithful.

Finding Courage

The Brits were discouraged. The war in Europe was drawing ever closer to their island home. Government officials saw no other alternative than to negotiate with Hitler. Hopelessness hung over England like a heavy fog.

But after Winston Churchill was elected prime minister, the mood of the English began to lift. In his first address to the nation, Churchill encouraged the people with these words: "Our task is to not only win the battle, but to win the war."[18] Hopelessness began to dissipate as the people realized their new prime minister intended to face the danger head-on.

On September 7, 1940, the bombing of London began. Massive amounts of property and many thousands of lives were lost. Englanders needed courage as never before. Against the advice of his cabinet and the pleas of his wife, following each bombing raid Churchill left his residence to personally survey the damage. When Londoners saw Churchill amidst the rubble, they were heartened. On one occasion, Churchill helped dig through the debris to find a woman trapped under her own home. On more than one occasion, Churchill wept as he came face to face with the suffering of his fellow countrymen.

Churchill's words, actions, attitude, presence, and empathy infused courage into the British people. Their resolve to preserve their country was deepened. The tenacity, courage, and determination of "the bulldog of England" became evident all over Britain.

The people found the courage to go on.

Our brothers and sisters in Christ can be encouraged by *our* active presence in their lives. We can speak words of truth and comfort to strengthen their hearts.

A young mother, pushing a stroller holding a crying baby and a sleepy toddler, visits a Mothers of Preschoolers group for the first time. She has never left her little ones in the care of someone she does not know. Overwhelmed with guilt for wanting time to build friendships with other women, she considers turning around and fleeing the church.

Before she has a chance to escape, a mentor mom approaches to introduce herself. Aware that the young woman is struggling with anxiety, the mentor explains the MOPS environment. The workers love children. They have cared for hundreds of babies and toddlers. They are all CPR trained and have had background checks. If your little one needs you, they will call you right away. This is good for you. You need some time to relax and refresh yourself so you can be the mom you want to be. We are happy you are here.

The mentor's reassurance gives the young mother courage. She leaves her children for two hours to learn, laugh, and build friendships. She returns to the nursery to find her toddler happily playing with blocks and the baby asleep in the arms of a caregiver. She feels refreshed for the first time in months. Though this may appear to be a small step of courage, it is one that can have a profound impact on the young mother and her family as she grows in her faith.

A declining church considers staff layoffs or drastic salary cuts. The pastor lies awake at night, wondering what he could have done differently. Surely, he thinks, this painful situation is his fault. Perhaps he misunderstood God's call to ministry. A dark depression creeps in. He talks to his wife about leaving ministry.

Then one day he opens his e-mail to finds a note from a college student he had mentored through a troublesome time. The young man thanks the pastor for standing by him, praying for him, and not judging him for struggling with his faith. Now, as part of a campus ministry, the student is finding joy and purpose in leading a Bible study on the gospel of John. None of this would have been possible without the pastor's encouragement. "Thanks for being there," he writes.

And the pastor finds the courage to go on.

We all face times of fear and discouragement. We all need each other to find the courage to go on.

The writer of Hebrews was the Winston Churchill of the early church. He understood there were many long years of toil and struggle ahead for God's people. They would need the encouragement of their brothers and sisters. The unnamed author (some believe it was Paul) urges believers not to neglect meeting together, but to be involved in "encouraging one another—and all the more as you see the Day approaching" (Hebrews 10:25).

Daily, our culture grows less friendly toward Christianity. The media desensitize people to unhealthy and unbiblical attitudes. We increasingly face direct challenges to our faith. We know we have many long months and years of toil and struggle ahead. Staying the course feels like an unreasonable demand. Finishing well seems impossible.

We stagger backwards, ready to fall. Who will catch us?

A brother of sister, of course. They will wrap their arms around us to help us, even, if need be, carrying us to the finish line while the rest of our family cheers us on.

Together, we will make it to the finish line. Because of the encouragement of fellow believers, we will shout the words of Paul: "I have fought the good fight, I have finished the race, I have kept the faith" (2 Timothy 4:7).

Encouraging Words Build Up

When he was nine years old, Ray dressed in a flowing white robe (a repurposed baptismal gown) and prepared for his grand entrance. He had been cast in the most sought-after role in the annual Christmas play—the angel. And he was about to deliver the most important line of all: "Fear not, for I bring you tidings of great joy!"

Convinced that practice makes perfect, he had rehearsed his line a thousand times. Perhaps he needed to say it in a deeper voice to convey the full weight of the angel's message. Or should he say it more slowly, with a greater emphasis on the first two words?

Ray remembers his performance well:

"I heard the long-awaited cue. Gliding onto the stage, ready to deliver the angelic message, I turned to see the sanctuary.

Of all things, it was filled with adults. They stared at me in anticipation. I froze.

"Not only could I not say my line, I no longer remembered a single word. My mind was blank, my stomach in a knot, my knees wobbly. Deafening silence.

"Eventually, a sympathetic adult standing off-stage bellowed, 'Fear not, for I bring you tidings of great joy.' My exit was not nearly as angelic as my entrance—I ran to the restroom and collapsed in tears.

"And so ended my budding stage career.

"This experience traumatized me as a nine-year-old boy. I reached the conclusion that speaking in front of people was *not* for me. I would do whatever was necessary to avoid such humiliation in the future.

"But Simon Johnson had reached a different conclusion. Simon, a patriarch in the church, loved Jesus and understood young people. Shortly after the Christmas play disaster, he approached me in the foyer of the church and put his hand on my shoulder. In his thick Swedish accent, Simon said, 'Ray, I think someday you will be a preacher.'

"I have often wondered what prompted him to say such a thing. I now know it was not *what* but *who*—the Holy Spirit. I have never forgotten Simon's words. His encouragement prompted me to consider a career path I might not have considered on my own. As a pastor, church planter, denominational leader, and church consultant, I have spoken before congregations in the United States, France, Estonia, Haiti, Japan, and the Philippines. I always experience a few butterflies when I get up to speak in a new setting, but stage fright is, for the most part, a thing of the past.

"That older believer's words built me up. His encouragement laid a foundation for future ministry. Over the years, others came alongside and added bricks and mortar to the foundation.

They offered encouragement, guidance, correction, and prayers, those things we all need to feel at home and serve effectively in the church."

As a boy in church, Ray experienced the truth of Proverbs 16:24 (ESV): "Gracious words are like a honeycomb, sweetness to the soul and health to the body."

"Building Up"

The Greek word in 1 Thessalonians 5:11 translated "build up" is often used in the New Testament for the construction of an edifice. It can mean to build or repair a house. It can also be used figuratively, in the sense of contributing to another person's advancement in religious knowledge. In Matthew 7:24, Jesus used this word in both senses, challenging His followers to build their spiritual house "on the rock."

The apostle Paul was directing us as believers to encourage and "build up" our brothers and sisters. We are asked to contribute in positive ways to their faith, moving them closer to Jesus one step at a time. When we build each other up, we add to the beauty and functionality of our fellow believers' faith. We make them feel at home in our presence.

This "building up" in the figurative sense is accomplished largely through what we say—so Paul urges us to speak carefully. "Let no corrupting talk come out of your mouths, but only such as is good for building up, as fits the occasion, that it may give grace to those who hear" (Ephesians 4:29 ESV). Our words can tear down, discourage, and damage other believers, or build up, repair, and enhance them. The choice is ours to make: "A word fitly spoken is like apples of gold in a setting of silver" (Proverbs 25:11 ESV).

According to 1 Corinthians 14, we also build up the church (which is made up of each of us as individuals) through the use of our spiritual gifts. In 1 Corinthians 13, the "Love Chapter," Paul had just reminded believers that love was their highest priority. He now encouraged these believers to use their spiritual gifts in love to build up the church.

No one was to be proud about their own gift. "What then shall we say, brothers and sisters? When you come together, each of you has a hymn, or a word of instruction, a revelation, a tongue or an interpretation." No, spiritual gifts were to be exercised for one reason and one reason alone: "Everything must be done so that the church may be built up" (1 Corinthians 14:26).

What good is it to have the gift of service, if there is no one to serve? Why teach, if there is no one to listen? Spiritual gifts are given to us to build up the church—both as individuals and a body—to the glory of God.

Just as any house construction requires the gifts of carpenters, plumbers, electricians, and painters, our spiritual growth requires the gifts of our brothers and sisters in Christ. We need teachers, encouragers, helpers, preachers, artists, leaders, and givers if we're all going to become the building God wants us to be. "So Christ himself gave the apostles, the prophets, the evangelists, the pastors and teachers, to equip his people for works of service, so that the body of Christ may be built up" (Ephesians 4:11–12).

I think of many people who actively build up the faith of their brothers and sisters. Small group leaders and members meet to study God's Word and pray—each person finds strength and encouragement as they share life together. Children's ministry leaders and teachers build up students each week—biblical teaching and words of encouragement are their tools. Generous givers help to provide staff and facilities that allow other believers to join in the building up of the entire congregation each week.

Our kind, intentional words and service create a church where everyone can make themselves at home.

Rebuilding

Building a house is a long enough process. But decorating and furnishing and keeping it in good repair is a lifelong commitment.

Eight years before I wrote this book, Ray and I built a town-home. Skilled workers put in hours of labor to create the home we wanted. Now, wear and tear are beginning to show on our place.

At year five, we replaced the element in the water heater. Year seven, a storm loosened some exterior siding. A few of the stone tiles in the kitchen have cracked and chipped from the house settling. We had to replace the garage door, not from wear but because someone forgot to open the door before backing out. (Do you think that is the "tear" part in "wear and tear"?) The dishwasher just died, and our plans to replace the cheapest builder's grade carpet with wood floors can be put off no longer. Two or three bushes from the original landscaping need to be replaced.

For our much-loved home's sake, we need to start the "building up" process again. To neglect it would be irresponsible, and possibly disastrous.

Building up our fellow Christians is not a one-time event, either. We have a mutual need for ongoing words of encouragement and acts of service. To neglect this ministry of encouragement would be irresponsible, and possibly disastrous. Sometimes the rebuilding is of a more serious nature and repairs need to be done on the very foundation of a believer's faith. It takes determination and perseverance to engage in such an intense process.

When we invest deeply in encouragement, we raise the likelihood that we will have healthy, affectionate relationships with our brothers and sisters in Christ. It also increases the likelihood that we will sense that we have finally found our spiritual home.

Encouragement was the name of the game for a Bible character called Barnabas. That was a nickname given to him by his fellow believers—his real name was Joseph, and he was a cousin of the gospel writer Mark.

In the book of Acts we read that he sold his own land to make a financial gift to the church. "Joseph, a Levite from Cyprus, whom the apostles called Barnabas (which means 'son of encouragement'), sold a field he owned and brought the money and put it at the apostles' feet" (Acts 4:36–37). Barnabas gave sacrificially to build up and encourage the church.

Also in Acts, we see Barnabas coming alongside (a biblical picture for encouragement) Saul in a time of need. The Jewish believers were wary of Saul, the Christian persecutor who was now making a profession of faith. Barnabas stepped in to vouch for the fledgling Christian, who would soon be known as Paul. Through Barnabas's encouragement, the disciples formed a strong bond to the man who would become God's apostle to the Gentiles.

If encouragement includes exhorting brothers and sisters to make it to the finish line, Barnabas fits the bill. "[The church at Jerusalem] sent Barnabas to Antioch. When he arrived and saw what the grace of God had done, he was glad and encouraged them all to remain true to the Lord with all their hearts" (Acts 11:22–23).

But we aren't done with our friend Barnabas quite yet.

In Acts 15, we discover that Paul, now firmly established as a Christian leader, was not eager to take John Mark—Barnabas's cousin—on a trip to revisit cities in which they had already preached. Earlier, the youthful John had left the mission to return home to Jerusalem. Paul may have considered the young man unreliable. Perhaps he had abandoned Paul when he was most needed.

Just as Barnabas had stepped in for Paul early in his ministry, he now stepped in for John Mark. Barnabas saw the potential in the young man, coming alongside him to give him a second chance.

Sadly, this disagreement caused the apostle Paul and Barnabas to go their separate ways in ministry. Yet, somehow—very possibly through the efforts of Barnabas—Paul ultimately came to forgive and restore John Mark. In a letter to Timothy, believed to be Paul's last, he wrote, "Get Mark and bring him with you, because he is helpful to me in my ministry" (2 Timothy 4:11).

Barnabas earned his nickname. In every way, he was an encourager. He encouraged believers in their newfound faith. He encouraged the early church with his own sacrificial giving. He encouraged the skeptical disciples to accept the new convert Paul. He encouraged a young man—who would go on to write a gospel account—by giving him a second chance in ministry. Barnabas built up and rebuilt.

Some, like Barnabas, have the gift of encouragement. They are my favorite people. Encouraging words and acts of service are fuel for effective ministry. Encouraging words infuse us with the energy to go on. We need encouragers.

Even if we do not have the gift of encouragement, we are all called to encourage and build one another up. We too can be sons and daughters of encouragement.

When was the last time you felt at home in your church? Maybe that sense of love, belonging, and care was the result of an encouraging word.

Be Kind and Tenderhearted

> Be kind to one another, tenderhearted, forgiving one another, as God in Christ forgave you.
>
> Ephesians 4:32 ESV

Kindness is hard to define, but we all know it when we see it. The old saying is true: "Kindness is the language the deaf can hear and the blind can see." Kindness transcends all barriers of communication and culture.

Kindness makes us feel at home.

I can't think of anything more attractive and appealing than a church marked by kindness. Who wouldn't want to attend a kind church?

Did you have a favorite teacher in elementary school? A favorite aunt or uncle? What drew you to that person? Was she or he kind?

I asked our youngest daughter, Joy, to name her favorite teacher. "Mrs. Jackson, of course. She was always kind." Even when disciplining children, her voice was soft and her demeanor gentle. Her kindness and fun-loving attitude drew families to our small Christian school. Influenced by the kindness, patience, and consistency of their teacher, many children grew in their relationship to Jesus. The children felt safe and at home in Mrs. Jackson's classroom.

If I had a choice between a church with the latest technology and programming or one made up of sincerely kind people, the latter would win hands down. If we relocated and were looking for a new church home, it might not be the one with the cutting edge ministries that would win my heart. I am drawn to Christian kindness.

Lord, give me kind and caring brothers and sisters. That is what I really want. That is what I really need.

Kindness breeds love. When our hearts are touched by the kindness of a brother or sister, our love for them grows. Kindness is irresistible.

In our forty-plus years of ministry, Ray and I have been touched by an endless stream of kindness from our brothers and sisters in Christ. When we think of their kindness, our hearts are filled with deep affection for them, even though we are separated by many years, many miles, or difficult circumstances.

In our early days of marriage, a more seasoned ministry couple from church invited us into their home. We spent hundreds of hours with Miriam and Herald. Miriam taught me how to entertain large groups and shared her favorite recipes. Her kindness and encouragement helped to prepare me for my life as a wife, mother, and ministry partner.

Kind and encouraging words were offered as Ray began to preach and engage in full-time ministry. When our struggling church plant could not pay our full salary, an elder showed up at our door with an armload of groceries. I spent three months on bedrest during our second pregnancy. The women of our church provided meals for our little family week after week, without complaint. Whatever doubt and discouragement we experienced in the ministry evaporated as we soaked up the kindness of these brothers and sisters.

I have seen kindness, even in moments of conflict. The effects are amazing: "A gentle answer turns away wrath" (Proverbs 15:1). Kind people are not only generous and thoughtful, but careful with their words. They do not react quickly or harshly. Their concern is for the feelings and well-being of the other person.

In the New Testament, the Greek word translated "kind" carries the meaning of gentleness. Someone who is kind is gentle and mellow, even in their words. The dictionary definition for *mellow* is thought provoking: to be mellow is to be "softened and made gentle, understanding, and sympathetic by age and experience."[19]

Wouldn't it be wonderful if as we aged we became mellower as Christians—softer, gentler, more sympathetic and understanding . . . if we became kinder? Kindness is the quiet, mostly unseen work of the church. Without kindness our relationships will fall apart. It is no wonder that Paul began his list of the attributes of love by saying, "Love is patient and kind" (1 Corinthians 13:4 ESV).

Tenderhearted Empathy

To be truly kind, we must be tenderhearted. When faced with a brother or sister's emotional and spiritual needs, a tenderhearted person takes action in positive and helpful ways.

Marriage expert and author John Gottman has interviewed thousands of couples for almost thirty years. His research has revealed the key to a happy marriage: empathy.[20] Couples who tenderly respond to one another's needs report high marital satisfaction. Even when a spouse cannot meet the actual need of the other, simply responding with kindness and empathy strengthens the bond. Kindness and empathy meet a deeper, more fundamental need of the human heart and draw people to each other.

Fellow believers showed me the value and beauty of kindness and empathy when Ray and I moved to France. Going there was difficult for me. As an introvert and the mother of four introverts, I was unsure how I would handle new people and places and things. My mind raced. Where would we live? Where would our children go to school? Would there be places for the children to play? Where would we shop? What about the language? (I rarely spoke aloud in groups here in the States—how would I ever make myself heard or understood in another language?) Would I be able to bridge the cultural barriers to make friends? What about ministry? Would I fit in? How would we all adjust?

I needn't have feared. Dennis and Barb Danylak came to our rescue.

As we packed our belongings in the States, this family of missionaries-in-training prepared an apartment for us in a suburb of Paris. Within a few weeks, they would finish their language training in France and move on to work with churches in the Ivory Coast.

Wanting to make our transition as smooth as possible, the five Danylaks moved out of their own apartment early, temporarily taking a smaller place. For the next two years, our family would call their larger apartment home. We could immediately settle into a new country and culture, and not worry about moving our kids a second time.

Barb and Dennis had gathered everything we would need to make our new life work. With our own belongings on a cargo ship somewhere in the Atlantic, the Danylaks set up tables, chairs, kitchen items, and most importantly, beds in advance of our arrival.

When we did arrive, Barb immediately invited our children to play at her home. Meeting other kids so quickly certainly helped our children. Dennis escorted Ray and me to the *supermarché* for our first shopping trip, introducing us to the wonders of milk in boxes and the joys of French biscuits coated in chocolate. Whatever we needed to know, this couple was ready to give suggestions, encouragement, or directions—like how to find IKEA.

Our friends understood the shock of moving to another culture, and they eased our transition. With the Danylaks' help, our first few weeks in France went smoothly. Soon we slid into the daily routines of life in France and they took their tender hearts to the Ivory Coast where they built up and encouraged many African Christians.

Barb and Dennis were kind, selfless, tenderhearted friends. They weren't seeking fanfare or applause for their efforts. They simply cared about another family's adjustment and wanted to help. They truly made us feel at home.

Jesus the Tenderhearted

Jesus too was easily moved by the needs and concerns of others. One time, in a town called Nain, Jesus saw a funeral procession.

A widowed woman's only son had died, and many from Nain were grieving with her.

When the Lord saw the woman, his heart went out to her. "Don't cry," He said (Luke 7:13). Then He proceeded, by His miraculous power, to bring the young man back to life.

Jesus also revived Lazarus, after an unmistakable display of tenderhearted compassion at the man's tomb. "When Jesus saw [Lazarus's sister Mary] weeping, and the Jews who had come along with her also weeping, he was deeply moved in spirit and troubled. 'Where have you laid him?' he asked. 'Come and see, Lord,' they replied. Jesus wept" (John 11:33–35).

Jesus showed His tender heart by caring for His disciples. After sending out the Twelve, they returned to Jesus eager to share all that had happened. At the same time, crowds were clamoring for Jesus's attention. The commotion was so great that the disciples could neither eat nor rest. Concerned for their welfare, Jesus said, "Come with me by yourselves to a quiet place and get some rest" (Mark 6:31).

They pointed their boat toward a secluded place, but the throng, desperate to hear from the teacher, made an educated guess of His destination and ran ahead. When Jesus landed on shore, he found a large crowd waiting and "he had compassion on them, because they were like sheep without a shepherd. So he began teaching them many things" (Mark 6:34).

Jesus was tenderhearted toward people in any kind of need. During the last supper, when Jesus sent Judas out to do his work of betrayal, many assumed Jesus had sent him out to give a gift to the poor. We can guess it may have been the custom of Jesus and His disciples to share their resources with the hungry and homeless (John 13:29).

To be kind and tenderhearted toward one another may seem unimportant. Yet the example of Jesus's selfless kindness and compassion demonstrates the power of kind words and actions.

Every day we make a conscious choice whether to be kind or hardhearted. Like the popular pastor and author Max Lucado, we can choose: "I choose kindness . . . I will be kind to the poor, for they are alone. Kind to the rich, for they are afraid. And kind to the unkind, for such is how God has treated me."[21]

Who needs your kindness today? In the church, your kindness and compassion will make both believers and non-believers feel at home.

Forgive One Another

During the American Civil War, the compassionate work of Clara Barton earned her the nickname "angel of the battlefield." From an early age, she would help anyone in need. When just a young girl, she pitched in to paint and repair the home the Barton family lived in. At the age of ten, she helped to care for a brother who had suffered a head injury.

Her tough-mindedness and determination paved the way for her to be the first woman to work in a combat zone. At the end of the Civil War, Clara worked for the US War Department. The bloody conflict had displaced many families, and Clara helped soldiers find and reunite with their loved ones.

In 1881, she founded the American Red Cross. Clara Barton was a gutsy, fearless woman. But that doesn't mean she was hard and cold.

One day, a friend brought up a painful injustice that had been done to Clara years earlier. The friend rehearsed the details of the incident but, strangely, it seemed Clara was drawing a blank. She had no recollection of the heartbreaking event. "Don't you remember the wrong that was done you?" her friend asked. "No," came Clara's reply. "I distinctly remember forgetting that."[22]

Can we forgive and forget? Maybe the better question is this: Even if we can't completely forget, can we forgive? Yes, we can.

Forgiveness is a choice. It is a matter of obedience. We are able to forgive others because God has forgiven us. He gives us a clean slate; we give a clean slate to others. He doesn't hold a grudge against us; we don't hold a grudge against a brother or sister. He doesn't dredge up our sins; we do not recall the sins of others. We choose to let them go.

Author Anne Lamott puts it this way: "Forgiveness means it finally becomes unimportant that you hit back. You're done."[23] When we forgive, we truly are done. Done reliving the event. Done with lying awake at night. Done with treating the person as if the offense occurred yesterday. Done with gossip. Done with darting out a side door to avoid our nemesis. Like Clara Barton, we choose to forget. We replace resentment and bitterness with memories of God's great love and forgiveness for us.

To be sure, forgiveness is hard work. It begins with a choice: we can choose to travel the same path Jesus did, the path of forgiveness and grace—or we can choose the world's path of revenge and angry feelings. One path leads to life and relationship. The other leads to bitterness and isolation.

Withholding Forgiveness

Some families struggle with forgiving. They hold on to grudges for years. A remark made at Aunt Mary's funeral can be dug up thirty years later at Grandma's wake. Refusing to offer forgiveness is a damaging family dynamic. No one feels at home because of the fear and resentment.

Some church families are dying from lack of forgiveness. Sins are routinely dug up and displayed for all to see. Grudges are fed and cherished. Slights are magnified into catastrophes. Growth is impossible when church members are held hostage by the past.

The news reports read like a movie script: on Sunday, April 27, 2003, in the tiny town of New Sweden, Maine, someone put arsenic in the coffee at Gustaf Adolph Lutheran Church. Sixteen people were hospitalized, and one died. Some of the congregants, most of them elderly, suffered long-term health effects.

Five days later, a member of the church was found dead of an apparently self-inflicted gunshot wound. There was a report of a suicide note that claimed responsibility for the poisoning, but police officials wondered if someone else may have been involved. Though at the time several church members told reporters that there was nothing beyond typical business meeting disagreements, a 2005 book about the case played up "bizarre accusations of conspiracy, revenge, and blood feuds."

Whatever happened at the Gustaf Adolph church, many churches do struggle with bitterness, grudges, and poisonous unforgiveness. The only answer for such destructive attitudes is biblical forgiveness. When we forgive, we refuse victimhood. We choose to focus on the grace of God—the grace that He's shown to us, and the grace that we in turn should share with others. We value mercy, grace, and the steadfast love of God above our own rights.

Of course, forgiveness is difficult. We are not like God, who forgives instantly and completely. But if we want to obey in this realm of forgiveness, He will give us the grace and power to follow through. As we allow God to work through us, we reflect His love and kindness to the world: "Who is a God like you, pardoning iniquity and passing over transgression for the remnant of his inheritance? He does not retain his anger forever, because he delights in steadfast love" (Micah 7:18 ESV). And we create a safe environment where our brothers and sisters in Christ feel confident and at home.

(As a counselor, I want to offer a brief word of caution here: while God does call us as Christians to forgive others, He does not demand that we stay in abusive, manipulative, toxic relationships. If your brain's alarm system is saying "get out," please listen to it and find help.)

Bless, Do Good, Pray

In most relationships, we work through our conflicts and reconcile. We know that forgiveness is real. Yet awkward and cold feelings can still ambush us. We wonder if we have truly forgiven. If we have, why can't we forget? Why is it that we want to avoid any interactions with the other person?

In many cases, we have truly forgiven. But even when forgiveness is genuine, we can expect to have lingering, uncomfortable feelings. These emotions can serve as a reminder of our need to keep our feet on the path of forgiveness. We need to cling to our decision to forgive.

Author and therapist Everett Worthington, in a teaching for the American Association of Christian Counselors, describes unforgiveness as a cold emotion. The secret to moving forward in forgiveness, according to Dr. Worthington, is to find ways to replace the cold, negative emotions of unforgiveness and resentment with warmer, more positive emotions of empathy and compassion. Perhaps Jesus's words in Matthew 5:44 (KJV) can help us: "But I say unto you, Love your enemies, bless them that curse you, do good to them that hate you, and pray for them which despitefully use you, and persecute you."

Love. Bless. Do Good. Pray.

It's a very tall order, but by personal experience I can tell you it works. When I consciously choose to bless, do good to, and pray for someone who has hurt me, I find that my emotions often soften and forgiveness comes more easily.

And if these attitudes apply to our enemies, how much more should we do these things for a brother or sister who has hurt us?

When we *love* a brother or sister who has offended us, we choose not to allow the offense to change the way we treat them. Just as we did not earn God's love, our brother or sister doesn't need to earn ours. We do not cut them off, but show the same demeanor to them as we do to the other members of our family. When we see this person walking toward us in the sanctuary, we don't avoid them—we acknowledge them and speak kindly to them. We treat them as God has treated us, and we do so by choice.

When we *bless* someone, we speak well of that person. No matter how the person has hurt us, we find positive things to say. And when we do, we recognize there is more to this person than the conflict. Blessing another with kind words highlights the good in the relationship. In time, the hard feelings begin to subside. We may even find that warm feelings, feelings of appreciation and even love, begin to take their place. When we bless, it is an act of love.

How do we *do good* to someone who has hurt us? When a tragedy strikes, we may be the first to arrive at the hospital or his home with offers of help and support. Perhaps the offender is moving—we can do good by carrying boxes or preparing a casserole. Did she lose her job? We call to express concern. Has illness struck his family? It is easy to send a get-well card or prepare a plate of cookies. Carpooling, running an errand, or doing a load of laundry are all opportunities for unselfish acts of service. Not easy, but with God's help we can do good.

When we do good, positive feelings rise to the surface. We reframe the relationship in spite of our hurt, creating new, more positive memories of our interactions. Our efforts affirm our intent to love and forgive, and that's helpful not only to the other person but to ourselves as well. Joy begins to creep into our lives, melting the edges of our once frozen soul.

And Jesus encourages us to *pray* for anyone who hurts us. This is the most powerful tool we have for changing our own perception. Praying takes the focus off of ourselves and our pain, putting it where it needs to be—on God and the other person's needs.

We will be tempted to pray that the other person will understand their part in the conflict—or even suffer consequences for their wrongdoing. Resist those thoughts. Self-centered prayer won't change our feelings toward our erring brother or sister. Licking our own wounds never moves us forward.

Try this: pray for God's blessing on the other person's life. Pray for health and safety. Pray that God will bless their work. Pray for loving friendships. Pray for their children. Pray that their relationship with Christ will flourish.

Before long, our first memory of the offender won't be the pain of the conflict, but of the selfless prayers we have offered on their behalf. We may never completely forget the wrong done to us, but like Clara Barton we can choose to replace bad memories with grace and forgiveness.

A church community characterized by these qualities is welcoming and safe. It is a place we can truly call home.

The Quiet Work of the Church

My friend Jan is the queen of illustrations. Everyday events and objects inspire her to consider and share spiritual truth. Her gift has enriched my life.

One day, she asked me, "What is the most important part of a wedding dress?" I was stumped. Thinking over our daughter's recent wedding, it seemed that *every* part of the dress was important . . . hours in the bridal shop made that clear. The fabric, the beading, the lace, the train, the veil were all important factors in our daughter's choice.

I offered several guesses to Jan's question, but she said they were all wrong. "It's the stitches. The stitches hold it all together," Jan stated. "The same is true of the church. It is the little things that hold it all together."

Things like kindness, empathy, and forgiveness are the quiet work of the church. Building people up with our words is rarely applauded. Banquets aren't given in the name of empathy.

Forgiveness is generally a private matter. But these small, quiet acts bring beauty to our church experience. Without them, we would fall apart.

Could it be that these are some of the righteous acts of God's people, as described in John's vision of heaven in Revelation 19:7–8? "'Let us rejoice and exult and give him the glory, for the marriage of the Lamb has come, and his Bride has made herself ready; it was granted her to clothe herself with fine linen, bright and pure'—for the fine linen is the righteous deeds of the saints" (ESV).

Kindness, empathy, encouragement, and forgiveness can adorn our church relationships like the lace and beads of a wedding dress. And then our church is not only a place to make ourselves at home, it's truly beautiful as well.

BRINGING IT HOME

- Who has helped you to cross the finish line? Who have you carried when they couldn't go on? Is there someone in your small group or church that could use encouragement right now?

- Consider the young people in your church. What gifts and potential have you noticed in each one? What can you say to encourage each one?

- Building up one another is important for all ages. Think of an older person in your church who needs encouragement. What can you do to break this person's fall?

- How gentle and kind are you? How concerned are you with the feelings of brothers and sisters in Christ? How do you express that kindness? Ask God for a tender heart for your spiritual siblings.

- How are you doing with forgiveness? Are you holding any grudges? Are you done with gossip? How often do you review offenses? If need be, seek a godly friend's help to forget the offense and remember the grace of God.

- Kindness, empathy, and forgiveness are "the quiet work of the church." Who could you thank for quietly working behind the scenes in your life?

6

Serve One Another

Using Our Gifts

Each of you should use whatever gift you have received to serve others, as faithful stewards of God's grace in its various forms.

1 Peter 4:10

Ministry takes place when divine resources meet human needs through loving channels to the glory of God.

Warren Wiersbe

I shuffled into Milwaukee's airport at the end of twelve stress-filled days. Ray's plane was due to arrive soon, bringing him home from the Philippines and Japan. While he'd been gone training pastors and church leaders on the other side of the world, a lot had happened here at home.

Our daughter and her husband had received news of a baby boy needing an adoptive home. His sudden arrival was a joy, but many questions remained about the legal aspects of the process. Meanwhile, everyone in our little clan had spent almost two weeks with fevers and coughing—always a concern to a grandma. I lost count of the times I'd visited the drugstore for Tylenol or cough medicine.

It was time for Ray to come home.

I was early for Ray's flight, so I decided to stroll through the airport lobby. I heard beautiful music that I soon realized was not coming from the overhead speakers. In the middle of the relatively small airport was a platform holding a black, polished grand piano. A young man was playing some familiar tunes with great expression.

As I walked by the video boards to check on Ray's arrival time, the young man began to play "Revelation Song." I stopped for a moment in front of the platform, smiled at the pianist, and whispered, "That is one of my favorites." He returned my smile and I had an instant understanding that we were both believers. I found a seat nearby, and for the next ten minutes, the young man played hymns and worship songs with great feeling and beauty. It felt like a mini-concert, just for me. My stress lifted as I was reminded of the omnipresent God who knows just what we need when we need it. For those few moments, I somehow felt at home, even in Milwaukee's airport.

Simple, unexpected acts of service can be such a blessing, even to people we don't know and in places we don't frequent. We typically think of "church" in terms of a particular building. But the church is not a building—it is composed of all those people who have chosen to follow Jesus and have experienced His saving grace. Serving one another is not confined to a particular place or time.

When someone senses a need in another person's life and attempts to meet that need, in some way—simple or profound—both are blessed. Why then does "serving" or "being a servant" have such a negative connotation for many people? I believe one reason is that we would often prefer others to serve *us*.

Serving Begins with the Right Attitude

I find myself falling into that trap. When the food I order in a restaurant is not presented to my satisfaction, I have at times blamed the server—the person who took my order and brought me my food. Of course, the server was not the person who prepared the food, but the one who was easiest to blame—the one I would expect to solve the problem. But, in all honesty, the problem may have started with me. I may have misread the menu or didn't understand what I was ordering or failed to clarify the changes I wanted in the way my meal was prepared.

This is an attitude that can carry over into the important relationships in our lives—even our relationship with the Lord. Often we have expectations that we expect *God* to fulfill, as if He exists to serve us rather than us serving Him.

Even Jesus's disciples occasionally struggled with this way of thinking. Near the end of the Lord's ministry on earth, James and John approach Him with an extraordinary request: "Teacher . . . we want you to do for us whatever we ask" (Mark 10:35).

I don't know about you, but as a parent and grandparent, I have learned to be wary of requests like that! Somehow, it seems they always involve spending money I don't have, making a promise I can't keep, or maybe dressing up in a silly costume.

Jesus knew what was coming, but He responded graciously. "What do you want me to do for you?" He asked.

Here it comes: "Let one of us sit at your right and the other at your left in your glory," the two sons of Zebedee answered (Mark 10:36–37).

As Jesus described His own impending arrest, abuse, and execution, all they could think about was their own self-importance. When the other disciples learned of James and John's request, they were, not surprisingly, "indignant." It was time for Jesus to call a huddle and explain to His team the nature and attitude of a servant. And, not surprisingly, He used himself as the example of what it means to serve others: "Whoever wants to become great among you must be your servant, and whoever wants to be first must be slave of all" (Mark 10:43–44).

What? That's not the way things work, not even for fisherman in the first century. What in the world is Jesus talking about? Somebody has to be in charge!

Then He delivers the zinger: "For even the Son of Man did not come to be served, but to serve, and to give his life as a ransom for many" (Mark 10:45).

Jesus is the exception to the perception. He did come to serve us, but not in ways we might imagine. He understood the real need of the disciples, and of us today: to be delivered from the power of sin and presented as faultless before our Creator. Jesus understood that only He could accomplish that—and He would have to become a servant to make it happen.

By His extraordinary life of service and sacrifice, Jesus provided the model for all disciples to follow, whether the original Twelve or the untold millions of us today. Serving one another lies at the heart of a relationally healthy family, and at the core of a relationally healthy church.

The apostle Paul understood that as he wrote to the church in Philippi, warning the people against "selfish ambition," "vain conceit," and "looking to our own interests" (Philippians 2). He reminded them of the Lord's model: "Have the same mindset as Christ Jesus: Who, being in the very nature God, did not consider equality with God something to be used to his own advantage; rather, he made himself nothing by taking the very nature of a servant, being made in human likeness" (Philippians 2:5–7).

Volumes have been written about the nature of the incarnation, the process of Jesus becoming fully human while remaining fully God. The author of creation entered the world in the very flesh He designed for us to inhabit. The God who is not affected by time, hunger, thirst, or pain endured all of these things to make a way to restore humanity's relationship with its creator. There is no greater model of serving others than what Christ did for us.

Throughout the years Jesus spent with His disciples, this model of service was repeated over and over again. At the wedding feast in Cana, He fulfilled His mother's request to provide wine. He fed multitudes of people who gathered to listen to Him teach. Just before He went to the cross, He gathered His disciples in an upper room and, despite their objections, washed their feet. Then, in one final act of putting the greatest needs of others before His own, He was killed on a cross to pay the price for human sin.

After Jesus's resurrection, He showed His friends—who had vainly fished all night—where to cast their nets. After they had made a miraculous catch, they returned to shore to find that Jesus had prepared a fire and cooked some fish and bread so they could have breakfast with Him.

Our gratitude for the humble service of Jesus should prompt us to serve our fellow believers in any way we can.

Serve with the Tools God Gives

Our son-in-law Justin has yet to meet a home improvement challenge that he fears to tackle. As father of three active kids, Justin saw that the carpeting in the family room was taking a beating. So he set about the task of researching, purchasing, and installing a hardwood floor.

But now the beautiful new flooring in the family room made the linoleum in the kitchen look shabby. So Justin decided to replace it with stone tile. Rather than work around the island cabinets, he decided to relocate them—*and* replace the countertop with granite. He had never tackled projects like this before, but Justin completed them with amazing results.

Over the years, Justin has collected many tools for such work. He has learned what anyone who attempts home improvement discovers: having the right tool for the job can reduce a lot of frustration.

We might be tempted to excuse ourselves from Christian service because "we don't have the tools"—we don't have the power Jesus had to turn water into wine or to feed more than five thousand people with a few loaves and fishes. That's true, but Jesus probably hasn't called you to perform miracles. The fact is, Jesus has supplied us with all the tools we need to serve one another. And we don't need to borrow or buy them, because He *gives* them to us.

Sadly, many believers leave their spiritual tools unused, still wrapped in their spiritual boxes. And the church is the poorer because of it.

I'm reminded of our family Christmas celebrations. They don't always occur on December 25, but there are usually a few hours sometime during the season when we can all be together. As more and more grandchildren become part of the mix, the excitement grows when it comes time to open presents. I can't imagine a Christmas when a single present is left unopened! The joy is just too great to overlook even one gift.

I believe that is one of the reasons God has granted us spiritual gifts—to discover the joy of serving others in ways that will help them grow in their faith. What a beautiful thing it is when we use our gifts to serve our brothers and sisters in Christ! It is a foundational key for unifying our churches.

In Ephesians 4, the apostle Paul describes the beauty of the body of Christ, that worldwide collection of every true believer, as God designed it to be. Paul emphasized that our use of spiritual gifts is essential for both unity and growth in the body, which includes our own local church congregations. These gifts were not designed to bring attention to ourselves, but to exalt Christ.

I love the word Paul uses to describe these gifts: *grace*. "But to each one of us grace has been given as Christ apportioned it" (Ephesians 4:7).

Perhaps a simple definition of spiritual gifts will help us understand them in the realm of serving others: *Spiritual gifts are special abilities, distributed by the Holy Spirit to every believer according to God's design and grace, to be used for the common good of the body.*

Let's look at the parts of this definition in more detail.

Special abilities: We don't serve other people out of our natural abilities, but by the special power that comes from God. As God works through us in the lives of others, our service always points back to Him.

Distributed by the Holy Spirit to every believer: God empowers every true Christian with at least one gift through the power of the Holy Spirit. It is not a few leaders—pastors, elders, teachers—who receive these gifts, but every follower of Christ.

For the common good of the body: The gifts are not designed to enhance the individuals who receive them. God gives these gifts so we will help others within the church, "so that the body of Christ may be built up until we all reach unity in the faith and in the knowledge of the Son of God and become mature, attaining to the whole measure of the fullness of Christ" (Ephesians 4:12–13).

That's pretty amazing when you stop and think about it! Spiritual growth in the church depends on each of us, as believers, using the gifts God has given us to serve one another. Each gift has a purpose—and since no one person has all the gifts, we truly need each other to grow in Christ.

Here is where, historically, the separation of clergy and lay people has created a great misunderstanding as to the nature of the body of Christ. "Ministry" was often seen as the work of professionally trained clergy. But that misses the true meaning of Pentecost. With the coming of the Holy Spirit in Acts 2, all believers—including those we now call "lay people"—were empowered to be a channel of God's power in the lives of others.

Ministry involves introducing people to Jesus for the purpose of reconciling them to God (2 Corinthians 5:11–18), and bringing them into the fellowship of the church. It continues as we nurture them in their growth toward spiritual maturity, using the gifts with which we have been entrusted.

The local church is more than the sum of its individual parts. Paul uses the uniqueness of the human body to help us understand this (1 Corinthians 12:12–31). Each member of the local church is like a part of the human body—feet, hands, eyes, and ears. Paul points out that all of the parts, though distinct, are part of the whole body—inseparable and interdependent. A foot cannot say, because it isn't the hand, that it is not part of the body. And no part of the body can say to another, "I don't need you!" (v. 21). Makes sense, doesn't it? In church terms, we can't deny that we have a connection to others simply because we don't want to be involved in their lives.

Sadly, that is how many of us live. Sometimes this attitude is construed as "the American spirit of independence," or anywhere in the world as "the self-made man" (or woman). It is almost countercultural to assert we aren't designed to live life in isolation and independence. Some of us feel isolated from other believers because we are different. Sometimes we play the comparison game, thinking we are better or worse than our fellow believers. But Paul would again provide the example of our physical body: "those parts of the body that seem to be weaker are indispensable and the parts that we think are less honorable, we treat with special honor" (1 Corinthians 12:22–23).

In our own way, we each struggle with pride in this area, and pride affects us all differently. It can cause some to want to be the center of attention, to exercise the more public gifts of preaching, teaching, and leading worship. Or, if we have less visible jobs—as nursery workers, caretakers, encouragers, or givers—it may drive us to envy the up-front people. Or our pride might prompt us to believe the lie that we don't need anyone else in our lives to help us grow in Christ.

Pride can keep us from using what God has given us, from delighting in the spiritual growth of others. It will never give our churches the homey atmosphere that people long to experience.

The Service Toolbox

While there is no single, exhaustive list of spiritual gifts in the New Testament, several passages describe tools God provides for serving one another in the church. We can put those gifts into a few common categories to help us understand the many ways God desires to use us.

Leading. Some of the gifts fall into the category of leadership. They are the special abilities some individuals have to allow the work of the church to be done "decently and in order" (1 Corinthians 14:40 ESV). Put negatively, these skills prevent chaos in the church! The apostle Paul wrote to the church in Rome that those gifted to lead should "do it diligently" (Romans 12:8). This would certainly include those gifted as apostles and prophets, and blessed with the gift of guidance (1 Corinthians 12:28).

I believe these are more than just "business skills." While the church is not a business, spiritual gifts of leadership enable a church to focus its ministries and resources on a clear vision and strategy for making disciples, and loving God and one another.

Godly leaders set a direction for the church that helps create an atmosphere where people can feel at home.

Nurturing and Caring. People with the nurturing and caring gifts are essential to any congregation serious about meeting the needs of people in the church and the larger community. These gifts include discernment (1 Corinthians 12:10), encouragement (Romans 12:8), faith (1 Corinthians 12:9), helping (1 Corinthians 12:28), hospitality and intercession (1 Peter 4:7–9), and mercy (Romans 12:8).

People gifted in leadership sometimes lack the nurturing and caring gifts necessary to perceive others' need or know how to meet those needs. That's why God provides such a diversity of gifts within the church!

The nurturing and caring gifts are essential to creating loving relationships and an atmosphere of caring in the church. People who have these gifts know how to make visitors feel at home. They make sure that newcomers are introduced to other people so they will find familiar faces when they return. Often, they provide the coffee and doughnuts so others can mingle and get to know one another. They love to connect people.

Instructing. Teaching people to become followers of Jesus and to grow into maturity in Christ is the church's mission. That's what Jesus said in some of His last words to the disciples, what we now know as the Great Commission: "go and make disciples of all nations, baptizing them in the name of the Father and of the Son and of the Holy Spirit, and teaching them to obey everything I have commanded you" (Matthew 28:19–20). God provides the gifts of teaching, knowledge, and wisdom to guide believers on their spiritual journey.

Throughout our ministry, we have learned that "head knowledge" is important—but it's not enough to transform people's lives. God has entrusted teachers with the truth of His Word and the instructing gifts that enable them to share the truth in ways people can understand and apply to their lives.

Don't think that this gift is limited to pastors or evangelists. One of the most common places for learning in churches today is the small group. These often meet in homes, an informal atmosphere where people can "share life together" as they study God's Word and pray for each other. Small groups allow people with the gift of teaching to minister in life-changing ways.

Inspiring. Many people today are inspired to worship and serve our Creator God by way of the arts—they want more than simply the teaching of facts. So people with gifts of creativity, craftsmanship, and other types of communication can help lift our eyes to the One "who is able to do immeasurably more than all we ask or imagine" (Ephesians 3:20).

People with these gifts augment a church's teaching, bring a new dimension to its worship, and turn our brick-and-stone facilities into places where God is glorified and both members and visitors can feel at home.

This is not an exhaustive list of the tools God provides to His followers. But it should be enough to give you a sense of how God provides us special enabling to do what He has called us to do in and through the local church. Not all service requires God's gifting—but using the gifts He's given us is great start toward finding our own place in the body of Christ.

Serving Together

We had four children in a relatively short time. When our youngest, Joy, was born, she was greeted by two-year-old Julie, four-year-old Jonathan, and six-year-old Jenny. The arrival of each child brought a new and unique dynamic to our home.

When the kids were newborns, they each required our full attention—and they got it! Each addition to the family meant that the older siblings gradually received less attention. As they grew, they were expected to do more on their own—clothe themselves, pick up their toys, take their dishes to the sink, let the dog out. (And occasionally put the binky back into the baby's mouth.)

Like most parents, we soon realized that none of our children were exactly alike. And that uniqueness could be challenging at times, especially as the kids got older. Our expectations might be easy for one child to fulfill, and nearly impossible for another.

This reality showed in their varying skills and abilities when it came to household chores. The simple command to "clean your room" often resulted in one child breaking down crying; one child starting the process but soon doing something else; one child carefully organizing things and putting them where they belonged; and one child completely disappearing.

We ultimately realized that our kids worked best in the areas of their strengths and abilities. When they teamed up on a project, and each could focus on his or her uniqueness, they got the most done. When they didn't work together, relationships were strained and much pouting, crying, yelling and blaming were heard. Even from mom and dad.

Of course, interpersonal struggles are part of living in a sinful world. But Satan loves to build on that natural tension, stirring up trouble both in families and among fellow believers in the local church. He knows that hurt feelings and divisions among believers can quickly destroy the reputation of a church, and reflect poorly on Jesus Christ. In the apostle Paul's letter to the churches of Galatia, he dealt sternly with their behavior and the effect it was having on their public character.

At one point he states the obvious: "If you bite and devour each other, watch out or you will be destroyed by each other"

(Galatians 5:15). Biting and devouring do not create the home Christ intended His church to be.

That behavior is reminiscent of people's lives before Christ, when they were in bondage to sin. Now, in the new life in Christ, they are set free from such behavior: "You, my brothers and sisters, were called to be free. But do not use your freedom to indulge the flesh; rather, *serve one another humbly in love.* For the entire law is fulfilled in keeping this one command: 'Love your neighbor as yourself'" (Galatians 5:13–14, emphasis added).

When we "serve one another," we are proactively engaging in behavior that counteracts the work of the enemy. That is the power of service! But notice the qualifiers Paul adds to the idea of serving: it should be done "humbly" and "in love."

To serve one another *humbly* is to recognize that only the power of Christ, who lives within us, enables us to affect people's lives positively, in ways that will help them to flourish spiritually. Apart from God's Spirit, we are equally capable of tearing people down and destroying them.

To serve one another *in love* means that we look after the other person's best interest, not our own. Because they are brothers or sisters in Christ, we are motivated to use the gifts God gave us to help them grow and experience His love in its fullness.

Your Part in the Big Picture

Perhaps you are seeing considerable overlap between the gifts of the Spirit and the "one another commands." What's the correlation between "practice hospitality toward one another" and having the gift of hospitality? People with the *gift* of hospitality have a special enabling to make visitors feel comfortable in their home, without pretense or showmanship ("hey, look how great *my* house is"). But all of us should *practice* hospitality as best we can in our church or at any special event our church might host.

Remember the big picture of God's plan: Jesus declared, "I will build my church and the gates of Hades will not overcome it" (Matthew 16:18). That means the church, not the enemy, will prevail in the end. God's church will win because He is empowering an army of believers to carry out His divine plan for restoring relationships for eternity. Christ in us is the hope of glory (Colossians 1:27).

It is in serving others, using the gifts God has given us in the power of the Holy Spirit, that we begin to understand what serving the Lord is all about. We begin to understand that life is not all about ourselves—our desires, our fame, or our comfort. Our lives should be about bringing life to others . . . and this makes our churches the kind of place people can make themselves at home.

BRINGING IT HOME

- How did God use other people to bring you to a personal relationship with himself? What spiritual gifts did you see (or do you now recognize) in their lives?

- How have others ministered to you in your journey of spiritual growth? What gifts did they employ to help you grow after your conversion?

- How has God used other people to help you feel at home in your current spiritual community? If you haven't experienced that feeling, what would you *want* other people to say or do for you?

- What gift or gifts do you sense God has given *you* to help others grow in their journey? How are you using those gifts to serve others in Jesus's name?

7

Confess Your Sins
and Pray for Each Other

Spiritual Bonding

I can no longer condemn or hate a brother for whom I pray, no matter how much trouble he causes me.

Dietrich Bonhoeffer

Therefore confess your sins to each other and pray for each other so that you may be healed.

James 5:16

Alone in Our Sin

Second Samuel 11 reads like a crime novel. The king, walking on the flat roof of his palace, sees a neighbor woman bathing. She is beautiful, and he is enticed. He longs for this woman, who he has no right to possess.

Adultery is a crime. But thinking he is somehow above the law, the king uses his position to obtain what his lust desires. It's not hard to imagine his thought process: "Surely, no one will ever find out. I am protected. I am the king."

But all of his plotting and conniving will backfire.

David's folly leads to an unwanted pregnancy with the wife of a man named Uriah. Now, the distraught king paces his chambers in fear, even desperation. What can he do to cover this sin? His choices will go from bad to worse, as he orders the killing of Uriah. One man is dead, a woman disgraced, and a king's leadership compromised.

The innocent baby conceived in the affair will die shortly after birth. And, most importantly, David's sin shatters his relationship with God. David will memorialize his agony in the psalms:

> When I kept silent,
> my bones wasted away
> through my groaning all day long.
> For day and night
> your hand was heavy on me;
> my strength was sapped
> as in the heat of summer.
>
> Psalm 32:3–4

In *Life Together*, the twentieth-century German theologian Dietrich Bonhoeffer wrote, "He who is alone with his sin is utterly alone."[24] Fortunately, God did not leave David alone in his sin. He sent the prophet Nathan to him.

Confess Your Sins to Each Other

David undoubtedly trusted this prophet. When David wanted to build a temple to house the ark of God, he discussed the idea with Nathan. Later, God gave Nathan a message to take back to the king: David would not build the temple, but his son Solomon would. David accepted the message that Nathan brought.

It would be Nathan who would approach David about his sin. Many months had passed since the king's adultery with Bathsheba. He'd had plenty of time to confess, but he had not done so. Though David admitted in the psalms that he was weighed down with the memory of his treachery and lust, it was clear now that he would need some prodding to make a full confession.

Nathan confronted David about his sin and its heinous cover-up. The prophet told the story of a rich man who stole a poor neighbor's beloved lamb to feed to guests. David was angered by the story, demanding the rich man pay for his sin—at which point Nathan said, "You are the man!" (2 Samuel 12:7).

The king was no longer alone in his sin. In the full light of Nathan's confrontation, David confessed, "I have sinned against the LORD." It was the beginning of his personal restoration.

Years later, David and Bathsheba named one of their sons Nathan (1 Chronicles 3:5), perhaps after the faithful prophet. Without his friend's loving honesty, David would have been utterly alone, his misery and broken relationship with God going on and on.

Are we any better than David? We too need friends to hold us accountable, and to encourage us on our road to recovery. We are not alone in our sin either, since we have our fellow believers. Like family, we support and help each other when sin overtakes us.

Easy Confession

In the 1970s, mini-revivals broke out spontaneously on the campuses of many Christian colleges. Normal chapel schedules were dismissed as students met not for one or two hours but for days. To God and to one another, they confessed their sins—lying, anger, withholding forgiveness, gossip, criticizing others, neglecting prayer, cheating, or lust. Sometimes they sought out people they had offended, asking forgiveness.

We were students at a Christian college during that time. I believe that most of these confessions were as sincere as the students' maturity allowed them to be. Young adults were humbly pursuing God with all their hearts.

In the decades that followed, I have been in sessions where confession was again encouraged. It is heartening to hear people honestly naming their struggles. "I'm too hard on myself," "I worry," "I'm a people pleaser," or "I'm too busy." These issues can cause pain and disrupt life. These battles can impede our spiritual growth. God has compassionate answers for these people, who need our love and support.

Is it possible that the Bible writer James was urging us to go even deeper in our confession? "Confess your sins to each other and pray for each other so that you may be healed" (James 5:16). There is a kind of confession that brings healing to our souls. What if we named our sins of materialism, anger, selfishness, complaining, and disobedience?

An old proverb says, "Confession is good for the soul." But at some point, an important word was left out. It should say, "open confession"—what I take to be humble and honest confession—is good for the soul. James encouraged believers to be open and honest with one another about their sin. Only then could they receive the love, support, encouragement, and accountability they needed for true healing.

Of course, the times, places, and people involved in our church confession should be considered carefully. But in appropriate times and ways, the confession James commands is an ongoing action. The verb tense he uses indicates we are to *go on confessing* our sins to one another, through the entirety of our spiritual journey.

So why is confessing our sins to one another so important? How does confession bring healing and build up the church?

Confession Requires Humility and Honesty

When we humbly and honestly share our struggles, faults, and sins with a trusted brother or sister in Christ, the door opens for growth. We give them permission to point out our blind spots. We accept their observations and suggestions. Our growth is accelerated as we absorb their godly input. The prayer support, accountability, and counsel of a concerned fellow believer draw us closer to Christ.

Confession provides opportunities for encouragement. Our trusted friends cheer us on as we get back into the race. They come alongside and help us make it to the finish line. When we hide our sins from others, we rob ourselves of this encouragement. We limit our opportunity for restoration and growth.

Confession helps us to appropriate forgiveness. When we hide our sin, we hide ourselves from what we most need—God's love and forgiveness. Our Christian brother or sister can remind us of God's promises to those who humbly confess. Humble, honest, and open confession can heal our souls.

And confession is good for the soul of the whole church. It is part of our wellness plan. When we humbly, honestly, and discreetly confess sins to our brothers and sisters, we make use of the body's "immune system." We protect every member and the Christian body as a whole. We move the church forward in health and holiness.

Hidden sin has destroyed many churches. Without honesty and humility, there is no growth. Without honesty and humility, there is no holiness. But an atmosphere of honesty, openness, and humility creates safety—we are confident that our spiritual family will not only hold us accountable but walk with us into forgiveness.

Perhaps this is why we have the story of David's sin in our Bibles. David sinned. David hid. David connived and covered up. David was confronted by a trusted friend. David confessed. David was forgiven and restored.

Confession Is the First Step toward Healing

We do a lot of patching in life. A little duct tape here. A little wood glue there. A coat of paint. A few throw pillows. We dress things up and make them look good even when they are actively deteriorating.

My father was a patcher. A week after his funeral, one of the grandkids stepped in a puddle of water in Dad's carpeted basement family room. Ray pulled off a piece of paneling, uncovering a rusted pipe. A steady flow of water was silently running down and under the wall.

We quickly realized that my father had been aware of the problem. Yards of duct tape and globs of plumber's putty on the old pipe revealed a longstanding problem. My mother recounted numerous trips to the hardware store for one more roll of tape and another can of putty. Clearly, patching didn't work. If only Dad had admitted the problem and called a plumber.

"The work of restoration cannot begin until a problem is fully faced," says author and counselor Dan Allender.[25] He was speaking of recovery from childhood abuse, but the words are just as true in connection with our own sins. We cannot heal until we face the real problem.

My husband is part of an organization that helps churches longing for greater impact in their communities. Often, these churches admit to relational and financial struggles.

One church reached out for help after barely surviving a conflict. It had lost its vitality. In fact, the place was gloomy.

But everything changed one Saturday when a coach from Ray's ministry taught on dealing with conflict in the church. What did he share with the church? The "one another" passages of the New Testament.

Church leaders suddenly realized the root of their problem was not financial. It was not the community's perception of their ministry. It wasn't the fault of other churches in the town. It wasn't their music or ministries.

They were their own worst enemy.

Unconfessed sin had created their misery. They were like David, after his failure with Bathsheba: "When I kept silent about my sin, my body wasted away through my groaning all day long. For day and night Your hand was heavy upon me; my vitality was drained away as with the fever heat of summer" (Psalm 32:3–4 NASB).

So, in honesty and humility, church leaders confessed their hidden sin: they had mistreated their previous three pastors. Each one fled the church, wounded and discouraged. In denial of the real issue, the congregation had tried patching up their suffering church with new strategies and ministries. A little duct tape here. A little putty there. Nothing worked.

Finally, they were ready to fully face the problem.

Courageously, the church invited its last three pastors to a reconciliation service. The one who chose to attend heard church members openly and humbly confess their relational sins toward him and his family. Forgiveness was requested—and granted. God worked. The reconciliation and restoration were real.

This one service didn't resolve all of the church's problems. But it did put them on a path toward greater health and holiness. It brought members closer together and created a more loving family atmosphere.

Confession Fosters Loving Relationships

To be accepted and loved by a Christian friend or mentor—in spite of our sin—generates feelings of affection, respect, and immense gratitude. To be trusted enough for someone to tell you their story of failure or struggle is a humbling, solemn, and holy honor.

After the confession of sin, it takes a great reservoir of love and courage to hold a person accountable. Many of us are tempted to give the person a hug and gloss over their wrong. It would certainly be easier just to encourage the brother or sister to move on. But when we truly care for our fellow believer's heart and soul, we are compelled to encourage, confront, and offer counsel when necessary. "Wounds from a friend can be trusted" (Proverbs 27:6).

Candid confession to a fellow Christian requires vulnerability and trust. The revelation of our wounded hearts can create a sense of intimacy and closeness. For this reason, it is wise for a man to confess to another man, and a woman to a woman. We must always remember that our goal is, first and foremost, the spiritual healing and holiness of fellow believer. Our interactions must always center on Jesus.

As we admit our flaws, struggles, and sins to one another, our relationships will flourish. Trust will be built. Friendships will grow. Each person will mature. "As iron sharpens iron, so one person sharpens another" (Proverbs 27:17).

Confession Ensures Honesty before God

In his classic study of Christian community, *Life Together,* Dietrich Bonhoeffer wrote eloquently on why confession to people ensures our honesty before God:

> Why should we not find it easier to go to a brother than to the holy God? But if we do, we must ask ourselves whether we have

not often been deceiving ourselves with our confession of sin to God, whether we have not rather been confessing our sins to ourselves and also granting ourselves absolution. . . . Who can give us the certainty that, in the confession and the forgiveness of our sins, we are not dealing with ourselves but with the living God? God gives us this certainty through our brother. Our brother breaks the circle of self-deception.[26]

In confessing our sins to one another, we are known completely. Our need to hide is gone. If we can be totally honest with another person, we are being honest with ourselves too—and ultimately honest with God. This is freedom.

In my counseling, I have had the privilege of meeting people who are seeking a place to name their sins. When a person audibly describes his or her sin, I can see their relief. Their vulnerability about their struggle is refreshing to me, and challenges me in the area of honesty. Most importantly, my counselees are ready to take the next step—to be honest with God. This is what healing looks like.

Can you name your sins to God? Do we even know what our sins really are? Can we be brutally honest to confess all the sin that so easily entangles us, or could hearing another person's confession stir a desire for greater honesty inside ourselves? The alternative is to minimize our sinfulness toward others and God, robbing ourselves of the freedom and joy He offers.

Healthy families understand the need for honesty. As we confess our sins to each other—with our brothers and sisters in Christ—we find healing in our church home.

Confession Brings Renewal

Many believers long and pray for revival in their churches. The idea of revival—a God-directed spiritual renewal—goes back to Old Testament times. How would you like to experience a revival like this one in Nehemiah's day?

"The Israelites gathered together, fasting and wearing sackcloth and putting dust on their heads. Those of Israelite descent separated themselves from all foreigners. They stood in their places and confessed their sins and the sins of their ancestors. They stood where they were and read from the Book of the Law of the LORD their God for a quarter of the day, and spent another quarter in confession and in worshiping the LORD their God" (Nehemiah 9:1–3).

Whenever God calls His people back to full devotion, it includes the confession of sin. Consider this often-quoted passage, 2 Chronicles 7:14: "If my people, who are called by my name, will humble themselves and pray and seek my face and turn from their wicked ways, then I will hear from heaven, and I will forgive their sin and will heal their land."

God provided a way for His Old Testament people to come back to Him, and He does the same for us today. We too can humble ourselves and pray and turn from our wickedness, just as the people of Israel could.

True revival comes when God's people join together in confession and repentance. In His grace, God has given us brothers and sisters in Christ to hold us accountable, to encourage our humility, and to challenge us to turn from sin and seek His face.

For New Testament believers who want spiritual healing for themselves, their church and the world, there is good news. There is a way back to God. We too, can humble ourselves, pray and turn from our wickedness just as the Old Testament believers did.

In His grace, God has also provided our brothers and sisters in Christ to hold us accountable, encourage our humility and challenge us to repent and seek God's face.

As we confess our sins to one another, we encourage the humility and repentance that are the conditions for real revival.

Confession Demands Prudence

If we are to confess our sins to one another, confidentiality is a must. To share the details of a private conversation given in this setting would not only be wrong, it could be devastating. It might damage the person's reputation. It could discourage them from seeking the help they need. The conclusion—it is dangerous to be honest—would be a logical one.

No wonder the Bible's book of Proverbs speaks to our speech: "A gossip betrays a confidence, but a trustworthy person keeps a secret" (11:13); "A gossip betrays a confidence, so avoid anyone who talks too much" (20:19).

When people confess their sins to us, they are entrusting us with very private information—essentially their very soul. We should guard that information more closely than a CIA agent protects state secrets. If we know ourselves well enough to know that we *can't* keep a confidence, then we have an obligation: we must say to our brother or sister that we are simply not in a place to hear sensitive matters.

Have you ever unintentionally let a very private word slip here and there? Have you ever heard (or ever said yourself), "I was told this in confidence, but I know I can share this with you—you won't tell anyone." If so, we need to confess these tendencies to a trusted friend who can hold us accountable and help us to grow.

If we had our own need for confession and accountability, we would certainly want a safe and trustworthy person to talk to. Here are some questions to consider when seeking a person to confess to . . . or asking yourself if you're the kind of person anyone else could trust: Does this person talk too much? Who do you know that intentionally refrains from gossip? Is he or she a new believer or a mature Christian? What Bible reading and prayer habits does this person have? Are you comfortable being around the person? Would he or she be judgmental? Do you suspect this person would seriously address, or excuse, your sin? Does this person possess the characteristics of wisdom as described in James 3:17–18? (You might want to ask a church leader for a recommendation of a person who would be a good partner for confession and accountability.)

What about *public* confession? Discretion is important. Know that this can cause pain for family members or friends of the person making the confession. It is worth asking yourself or the person you're helping, why? Will it be helpful to brothers and sisters in the church? Who could it hurt? Who might it confuse?

Sometimes, public confessions are meant to soothe one's own conscience or even to punish one's self. Neither are good reasons. But for larger, less common reasons—such as criminal behavior or sins against the body of Christ—public confession is appropriate.

Generally, public confessions come long after a private confession with a brother or sister. As we experience God's forgiveness and learn ways to overcome sin and grow in our faith, we may have helpful lessons to share along with the confession. Our admission of sin and testimony to God's grace adds something to the lives of our brothers and sisters. In those cases, a public confession is proof of God's power to transform.

Confessing our sins to each other reminds us that we all need God's grace. Christianity is a level playing field—we have all sinned. Today, I need your understanding, support, and encouragement. Tomorrow, you might need mine.

Because we are family, we give each other the grace and love that is needed when it is needed. In this environment, we can feel at home—and we can grow and mature.

Pray for One Another

After we returned to America from France in 1992, we occasionally heard from Daniel, one of Ray's faithful and enthusiastic church leaders in Menton. He always expressed concern for our family and never failed to convey the good wishes and affection of the congregation.

Almost ten years later, our oldest daughter, Jennifer, her husband, Michael, and their two small children spent a week in France. Jenny delighted in showing her husband the countryside and architecture of France. They ate roast chicken and French fries in familiar bistros. Four-year-old Nicole even ate escargot! At the end of the trip, Jenny took her little family to our former church, where our French friends showered them with love as only the French can do. They fussed over the children just as they had our own children years before. Jennifer felt like she was home.

Only days after returning to the states, Michael was killed in a motorcycle accident. He was only twenty-five.

We received hundreds of expressions of sympathy and condolence. But none meant more than a phone call from Daniel. Our friend was heartbroken for our family, especially for Michael's children. Daniel said the church sent its sympathy, but most of all he wanted us to know they would be praying.

We were thousands of miles away from these dear people. Yet, because of their prayers, we felt a comforting closeness to them. We were not alone. We were loved.

The German theologian Dietrich Bonhoeffer tells of preparing to leave his church in Berlin for another position in Barcelona, Spain. On his final Sunday, Bonhoeffer delivered the children's message with his whole heart. He was greatly saddened to say good-bye to the children, who he had spent two years teaching and loving.

At the end of the service, Bonhoeffer was especially emotional as he heard the children praying aloud for him. He wrote in his diary, "Where a people prays, there is the church, and where the church is, there is never loneliness."[27]

God works through the prayers of His people to bring comfort and strength. We are not alone when our brothers and sisters are interceding for us. "I always thank my God," the apostle Paul wrote to a friend, "as I remember you in my prayers" (Philemon 4).

Prayer Is a Necessity in the Church

King Herod had had enough, so he hatched an evil plan. Tracking down Peter and throwing him into prison (which history would indicate was a disgusting place) was the first step. Surrounding the apostle with four squads of four guards was next. This enhanced security would keep the rabble rouser securely locked away until the end of the Passover. Then a public trial would humiliate this leader of the new sect of Jesus followers. Herod would send a strong message to the believers—they wouldn't want to meet the same brutal fate as their leader. Soon, Herod would be rid of this pesky faction.

While Herod anticipated the upcoming trial, he was unaware of what was happening behind the scenes: "So Peter was kept in prison, but the church was earnestly praying to God for him" (Acts 12:5). Did it help? Absolutely—the night before the trial, Peter was miraculously freed from the chains that bound him to two soldiers, and the prison that had been his temporary home.

Prayer was an essential part of early church life. The believers prayed for the furtherance of the gospel. They prayed for their imprisoned and persecuted leaders. They prayed for deliverance from persecution. They prayed for physical and spiritual needs. They prayed for the salvation of loved ones and their Jewish and Gentile neighbors. They prayed.

And prayer is still an essential part of church life today. We pray for the furtherance of the gospel. We pray for the imprisoned and persecuted believers around the world. We pray for their deliverance from persecution. We pray for the physical and spiritual needs of other believers. We pray for the salvation of loved ones and neighbors. We pray for the brothers and sisters in our own congregation who are struggling with illness, disappointment, or sin. We pray.

Prayer Reminds Us We Are Not Alone

In prison, separated from fellow believers, Peter must have felt alone—perhaps even forgotten. But he had not been forgotten at all. His spiritual family, people who loved him, gathered together to pray for Peter.

The apostle Paul constantly asked for the prayers of those he had visited, relying upon their concern for him even when he was far away. Paul was in Corinth—some 275 miles away—when he urged the Thessalonians, "Brothers and sisters, pray for us" (2 Thessalonians 3:1). In recounting to the Corinthians the hardships of his missionary journey, Paul admits he had despaired of life. Yet he had been delivered and knew God would continue to deliver, "as you help us by your prayers" (2 Corinthians 1:11).

The apostle John prayed for the physical and spiritual health of fellow believers. "Dear friend, I pray that you may enjoy good health and that all may go well with you, even as your soul is getting along well" (3 John 2). Paul said he did not stop praying that the Colossians would be filled "with the knowledge of [God's] will through all the wisdom and understanding that the Spirit gives" (Colossians 1:9).

Early Christians counted on the love, concern, and prayers of their brothers and sisters in Christ. Their survival and growth depended upon prayer. No wonder James wrote, "Is anyone among you sick? Let them call the elders of the church to pray over them and anoint them with oil in the name of the Lord. And the prayer offered in faith will make the sick person well; the Lord will raise them up. If they have sinned, they will be forgiven. Therefore confess your sins to each other and pray for each other so that you may be healed. The prayer of a righteous person is powerful and effective" (James 5:14–16).

In every challenge of life, whether physical, emotional, or spiritual, our brothers and sisters depend on our prayers. And you and I depend on theirs. None of us should ever be alone in our time of need.

Prayer Expresses Love

When I was in college, I did housework for Herald and Miriam Welty. Herald was the registrar and Miriam an administrative assistant at Fort Wayne Bible College. Every Friday, I vacuumed, dusted, and cleaned bathrooms. Sometimes I would bake cookies for my friends. Miriam and Herald treated me as an adopted daughter. When I think of these godly people, I am still overwhelmed with the love and care they expressed to me.

They made me feel completely at home.

One Friday afternoon, I lifted Miriam's green, leather-like copy of The Living Bible from the coffee table. A piece of paper peeked from between the Bible's page—it was her prayer list. Toward the top, I saw my own name. Miriam had told me that she prayed for me. I never doubted her word, but seeing my name on her prayer list, tucked into her beloved Bible, was a thrill.

That was an upbeat moment in my life, a time when prayers are filled with joy and gratitude. But we all know there are times when we become so distressed, fatigued, discouraged, or filled with doubt that we find ourselves unable to pray. In those moments, we need someone who loves us to come alongside and pray on our behalf.

In his book *Stories for the Journey*, William White gives the account of a couple named Enid and Hans. They lived in Europe during the turbulent days of World War II. Hans loved teaching as a seminary professor. Fearing he would be removed from his position, he fled with Enid to America.

The adjustment to the culture and language was trying. They had left behind all that they had ever known and loved. Yet, in time, Hans regained his status as professor. Life was good once again.

The couple could be seen walking hand in hand across the campus. In church, they sat close, holding hands. Their loving relationship was noticed by everyone around them.

But the day came when Enid died. Hans was inconsolable, secluding himself for weeks at a time and forgetting even to eat. Friends and colleagues from the seminary visited Hans regularly, but nothing lifted his depression.

During one visit, Hans poured out his pain to four friends and colleagues. "I am no longer able to pray to God. In fact, I am not certain I believe in God." There was a moment of silence, until one professor responded. "Then we will believe for you. . . . We will pray for you."

And they did. Day after day they asked God to restore faith to Hans's heart. Just as a four friends carried a paralyzed man to Jesus (Mark 2:1–12), these friends brought Hans to God until his faith was restored.[28]

When we pray for our fellow believers we demonstrate both our faith in God and our love for one another. Intercessory prayer deepens our affection for others. And when that intercessory prayer is made on our behalf, we gratefully feel the love and care of our brothers and sisters. As the eighteenth-century English priest William Law wrote, "There is nothing that makes us love a man as much as prayer for him."[29]

Both confession and prayer allow us to enter into one another's lives in practical ways. We are able to demonstrate love, acceptance, forgiveness, and care—the very things that help us feel at home.

BRINGING IT HOME

- In the Bible, David experienced the heaviness of unconfessed sin. Reflect on times in your life when you could identify with his anguish. What would have been most helpful to you? Did you have anyone to whom you could turn?

- Are you tempted to engage in "easy confession"? What are the results of not being honest about our sin? How can we encourage honesty in our own confession and in the confession of our brothers and sisters?

- If a fellow Christian confesses his or her sins to you, how will you protect confidentiality? What boundaries will you put in place to protect you both?

- What do you think about revival? What is your part in the process of revival?

- The early church depended on the prayers of all believers, constantly meeting in one another's homes to pray: "They devoted themselves to the apostles' teaching and to fellowship, to the breaking of bread and to prayer" (Acts 2:42). How might praying for one another create an environment in your church that would make everyone feel at home?

8

Live in Harmony
with One Another

Making Beautiful Music

How good and pleasant it is when God's people live together
in unity!

Psalm 133:1

Live in harmony with one another.

Romans 12:16

*I*t began as an experiment. In 1972, cellist Julian Fifer pulled
together an ensemble of thirty-one musicians to create the
classical chamber orchestra Orpheus. During the orchestra's
four-plus decades, these exceptional musicians have recorded
more than seventy albums and received a Grammy for *Shadow
Dances: Stravinsky Miniatures*. Each season, they perform at

Carnegie Hall and dozens of other venues nationally and internationally. At times, they have been joined by Isaac Stern, Yo-Yo Ma, or other musicians of their stature.

What was the experiment? This orchestra performs without a conductor.

Julian Fifer's dream of musicians working together in a cooperative and creative way has come true. But it hasn't been easy. For a few years, the collaborative process was chaotic. Each musician hoped to share his or her individual interpretation. Moments of conflict were inevitable.

The solution to the problem was simple, if not easy: each performer had to listen more attentively to the others. In fact, Mr. Fifer estimates that 70 percent of rehearsal times are now spent with world-class musicians humbly listening to one another.

The goal of each musician is to enhance the performance of his or her colleagues, rather than seeking a personal limelight or stardom. When disagreements surface, the performers' common love of music wins out. One journalist played off of J. R. R. Tolkien's classic story to dub the group "The Fellowship of the Strings."[30]

By working in harmony with one another, these people make beautiful music. The apostle Paul instructed believers in Rome to "live in harmony with one another" (Romans 12:16). The command is just as applicable to churches today—and it is only when we live in harmony that we make the beautiful music of a happy home.

Imagine a church where each person's contribution is valued. Think how pleasant church would be if everyone listened respectfully and attentively to others, and each member was free to serve creatively without upstaging others or drawing attention to themselves. Do you dream of a fellowship where members humbly come together only to honor God?

While the goals of the church and of an orchestra differ greatly, we still can learn priceless lessons from the Orpheus ensemble. Careful listening, mutual respect, and sharing a common mission lead to greater harmony. Together, they create an environment where we can use our gifts, and feel valued and at home.

God and Harmony

The universe God designed functions in perfect balance and harmony. Scientists marvel at the precise equilibrium of the stars and planets, and the exact balance of elements within living things. This God-created harmony makes life possible.

The harmony that we see in God's creation is simply an extension of who He is. The three Persons of the Trinity have always existed in a harmonious relationship. The Father loves the Son. The Son obeys the Father and sends the Spirit. The Spirit works on behalf of both the Father and Son.

Outside of himself, God desires a harmonious relationship with humankind. Jesus came to reconcile us to God, to repair our discordant relationship with the Father. His work also mends fences between people—Jews and Gentiles, slave and free, male and female, including husbands and wives and members of families. And the harmony God designed us for should extend to His church.

My friend Nancy, who once worked with me on a church staff, exemplified this. I nicknamed her "Miss Harmony." *Harmony* was her primary quality on the Gallup StrengthsFinder test, but those of us who knew her didn't need a test to tell us that.

As the office administrator for a church of four hundred, Nancy's strength of harmony kept the ministry rolling. Every assignment was met with the same loving response. Every request deserved attention. Everyone was important. Nancy always listened and affirmed the needs of staff or congregation. She responded graciously, respectfully, kindly, and with a sense of humor. If she could not meet a need personally, she would work with the person to find other options.

When it was necessary to stand her ground on an issue, Nancy didn't hesitate—but she was always kind. Her goal was the welfare of our church.

When I want to respond appropriately to a particular situation, I think of Miss Harmony.

Disharmony in the Church

Not only does God love harmony, he hates discord. Proverbs 6 describes seven things that God particularly despises, like prideful eyes and a lying tongue. But the final entry on the list is a whole person: "he that soweth discord among the brethren" (v. 19 KJV). Or, as the New International Version says, "a person who stirs up conflict in the community."

Harmony is a foundational aspect of our church communities—not only is it taught in the Bible, we as believers need to agree that the Bible is our standard. Everything else builds upon that.

A Texas family built their seven hundred thousand dollar dream home on a cliff overlooking Lake Whitney. As they unpacked their belongings they must have thought, "Finally—we are home." But before long, they realized their house was shifting. The limestone cliff on which the home was built was developing an ever-widening crack; portions of the house were in danger of breaking away and tumbling seventy-five feet in to Lake Whitney. The family was evacuated and the house condemned. Eventually, the luxury home was burned to the ground to prevent the rest of it from sliding down the cliff and endangering people on the water below.[31]

The apostle Paul knew that discord could be a crack in the foundation for the early church. Any group of believers trying to build on divisiveness would eventually collapse or fall apart. Like that house on Lake Whitney, the collapse of a church through divisiveness could endanger many innocent people, spiritually speaking.

Early in 1 Corinthians, Paul addresses discord in the life of this Greek church. He was aware of divisions among the people, schisms that threatened their existence and witness. "I appeal to you, brothers and sisters, in the name of our Lord Jesus Christ, that all of you agree with one another in what you say and that there be no divisions among you, but that you be perfectly united in mind and thought" (1:10).

The word *united* in this verse can also be translated as "framed," "prepared," or "mended." Paul had in mind something that is perfectly whole, unbroken, not fractured or torn. This was the apostle's desire for unity in the Corinthian church.

Divisiveness was such a serious issue that Paul wrote to the church in Rome (and to us as Christians today) to avoid those who stir up conflict and fracture the unity of the church. "I urge you, brothers and sisters, to watch out for those who cause divisions and put obstacles in your way that are contrary to the teaching you have learned. Keep away from them" (Romans 16:17).

Paul used even stronger words in a letter to the young pastor Titus: "Warn a divisive person once, and then warn them a second time. After that, have nothing to do with them" (Titus 3:10). These are some of the harshest words in the New Testament.

Those who actively awaken discord, promote divisions, and rouse conflict in the church are to be disciplined in a very specific and serious manner.

God's plan calls for harmony in His church. Without harmony, none of us will ever feel at home.

Harmony over Leadership

The New Testament gives us a glimpse into some of the more common causes of discord in the church. The apostle Paul addressed disunity among the Corinthians.

Jumping fearlessly in to the fray, Paul said their divisions were based on individual allegiances to particular leaders. In fact, the loyalty of some Corinthian believers to Paul himself was part of the problem. Paul had a following.

Paul, always faithful to his mission, dealt with this in Corinth: "Is Christ divided? Was Paul crucified for you? Were you baptized in the name of Paul?" (1 Corinthians 1:13).

He was saying, "Wait a minute! I am not the source of your salvation. Neither are Apollos or Cephas. We are not in competition. We are all here to preach the gospel and to follow Christ with you."

Paul recognized that this fidelity to a particular person, left unchecked, could cause splinter groups in the church. That would compromise the spread of the gospel and endanger people's immortal souls.

This temptation to admire, follow, and swear allegiance to specific leaders is common. Many people find security in attaching themselves to a charismatic or well-known leader. Some are unwilling to tackle the task Paul urged on the Christians at Philippi: "to work out your salvation with fear and trembling" (Philippians 2:12).

The first chapter of 1 Corinthians ends with Paul reminding these discordant believers of how different God's view of the world is from sinful humanity's. The cross is foolishness to the world, Paul wrote, but to the saved, it is the power of God (v. 18). God calls few of the influential and powerful of the world, focusing more on the "foolish" and "weak" (vv. 26–27). Paul's point? "Let the one who boasts boast in the Lord" (v. 31).

As long as individual Corinthians kept a worldly focus on their preferred leaders, their relationships with each other would be out of tune. If they returned to the cross and followed Christ exclusively, their harmony would be restored. The beloved pastor and author A. W. Tozer pictured a church like that as a large collection of pianos:

> Has it ever occurred to you that one hundred pianos all tuned to the same fork are automatically tuned to each other? They are of one accord by being tuned, not to each other, but to another standard to which each one must individually bow.[32]

Disharmony Due to Pride

C. S. Lewis called pride "the great sin." In *Mere Christianity* he observed, "Pride is spiritual cancer: it eats up the very possibility of love, or contentment, or even common sense."[33]

The Bible's "one another command" about harmony speaks of laying aside our pride and prejudice: "Live in harmony with one another. Do not be proud, but be willing to associate with people of low position" (Romans 12:16).

Pride and prejudice in the church build barriers that isolate us from one another, with people refusing to acknowledge the inherent value of each person. They prevent harmony and damage our Christian witness. They take many forms in our churches.

Sometimes our prideful disharmony is based on appearance. We might decide whether we care to know another person by how she dresses or how articulate he might be. Have you ever seen or heard of a "sharp young couple" visiting a church, and quickly being pursued for leadership? This kind of prejudice is subtle and likely unintentional. Yet, when it occurs, unity and harmony are affected. Some people quickly have a higher status, but others with equally as much to offer may be neglected. James, the brother of Jesus, warned against this attitude:

> My brothers and sisters, believers in our glorious Lord Jesus Christ must not show favoritism. Suppose a man comes into your meeting wearing a gold ring and fine clothes, and a poor man in filthy old clothes also comes in. If you show special attention to the man wearing fine clothes and say, "Here's a good seat for you," but say to the poor man, "You stand there" or "Sit on the floor by my feet," have you not discriminated among yourselves and become judges with evil thoughts? Listen, my dear brothers and sisters: Has not God chosen those who are poor in the eyes of the world to be rich in faith and to inherit the kingdom he promised those who love him?
>
> James 2:1–5

Racial and ethnic prejudice in the church is one of the ugliest of sins. The gospel is the good news of reconciliation—of humanity to God and of one person to another. If we harbor racism, we plainly do not understand the gospel of Jesus Christ.

Racial reconciliation hinges on a change in our thinking that reflects the biblical story. Let's consider these truths and renew our minds with God's Word:

We are all made in the image of God. There are no exceptions to Genesis 1:26. We are all created in God's image and likeness. And God created each people group that carries that image with them wherever they called home. The sacred spark, present in each person, gives worth and value to all humanity and every individual. When we treat each other with the dignity and respect that the image of God deserves, we honor the Creator.

Jesus is our peace. "For he himself is our peace, who has made the two groups one and has destroyed the barrier, the dividing wall of hostility" (Ephesians 2:14). For centuries, there had been a dividing wall between God's chosen people (the Jewish nation) and all others (the Gentiles). The temple that existed during Jesus's earthly ministry had an outer court. Gentiles were permitted to enter the outer court but were forbidden from setting a foot in the inner courts—the holier areas of the temple. Signs in both Greek and Latin were posted, warning the Gentiles to go no further. The penalty for a Gentile breaching the dividing wall was death. When Christ invaded our world, He demolished every dividing wall. He made peace between God and man, and He made harmony possible between Jews and Gentiles. The two groups could now be one. They could worship together. No one was excluded. Human constructs that keep us from one another are no match for the reconciling power of Jesus Christ.

In Christ, there are no distinctions. "There is neither Jew nor Gentile, neither slave nor free, nor is there male and female, for you are all one in Christ Jesus" (Galatians 3:28). This couldn't be clearer: we are one in Christ. We have everything we need to live in harmony with one another in the church. There is no place for bias or prejudice.

And there are still other ways pride disrupts the harmony of our churches. For example, spiritual pride is caustic, demoralizing and isolating believers from one another. As we have discussed earlier, God gives each of His children one or more spiritual gifts, some more public and others less obvious. When we showcase specific gifts, we send the message that speaking or teaching or leading is a sign of spiritual superiority. Elevating one gift over another fails to reflect the interdependence of the body, a principle clearly taught by the apostle Paul:

> The eye cannot say to the hand, "I don't need you!" And the head cannot say to the feet, "I don't need you!" On the contrary, those parts of the body that seem to be weaker are indispensable, and the parts that we think are less honorable we treat with special honor. And the parts that are unpresentable are treated with special modesty, while our presentable parts need no special treatment. But God has put the body together, giving greater honor to the parts that lacked it, so that there should be no division in the body, but that its parts should have equal concern for each other.
>
> 1 Corinthians 12:21–25

Our physical well-being depends on each part of our bodies functioning in harmony with all the others. Our spiritual well-being occurs in exactly the same way. When we consciously reject the pride that is so much a part of our human nature, we build healthy, well-adjusted churches—places where we can all feel at home.

Honor and Prefer One Another

The New American Standard Bible translates Romans 12:10 this way: "Be devoted to one another in brotherly love; give preference to one another in honor."

Two key words jump out of this text: *preference* and *honor*.

The Greek word translated *preference* means "to go ahead." When we "give preference" to someone, we step aside and allow that brother or sister in Christ to go first.

When we show *honor* to fellow believers, we acknowledge that they are worthy of respect, esteem, and high regard. We see them as Christ sees them: as precious people for whom He died.

Quick to applaud their strengths and accomplishments, we are motivated to see them recognized and appreciated. We honor our brothers and sisters with our words, attitudes, and actions:

We honor children by making room for them in the church. We place a priority on their care and education by what we say, and by how we spend our money.

We honor young people by encouraging, mentoring, and investing in their growth. We honor them for their potential as future leaders of the church and give them age-appropriate responsibilities and opportunities. We applaud each success.

We honor the singles of our church by attitudes that invite them into full participation in the church. We honor their God-given talents and affirm them for their priceless contribution to the family of God.

We honor the families of the church by holding the role of parents in high regard and providing supportive ministries. We affirm that family life is sacred, important for passing along the Christian faith.

We honor the older people of the church by refusing to marginalize them. We recognize that there is no expiration date on spiritual giftedness and embrace all that our senior members have to offer. We don't forget them.

We honor those who are in need by providing appropriate resources and care. We treat them with tenderness, affection, respect, and dignity.

We honor our leaders, especially those who preach and teach. We are grateful for their faithfulness and hard work on our behalf. In many ways, we express honor, respect, and gratitude to those who have served us well.

We show honor to all of our brothers and sisters in Christ, regardless of age, income, ethnicity, or status.

Inspired by the belief that each person is deserving of dignity, we seek to show preference and honor to our fellow

Christians. This makes for a church where every believer can feel at home.

Yielding to Others

A man drove down an unfamiliar country road. When he came to a narrow bridge, he noticed a "Yield" sign at the entrance. Looking carefully, he waited to proceed until he was certain there was no one coming from the other direction.

Later that day, the man traveled the same road on his return. When he came to the narrow bridge from the opposite direction, he noticed the same warning on this side of the bridge: "Yield." Once again, he made sure no cars were coming from the other direction, then drove safely over the bridge and home to his family.

Why two signs? Wouldn't one be enough?

Yielding—giving honor and preference to others—is a two-way proposition. Just as two signs were intended to prevent collisions and injury on a bridge, our commitment to two-way yielding—to giving preference to others—can save our churches from heartache and damage.

Do you know Diotrephes? He was nothing but trouble. I can imagine the apostle John throwing up his hands in frustration as he wrote how Diotrephes "loves to be first" (3 John 9). Then John went on to explain other aspects of this man's arrogant and self-serving behavior: he would not welcome John and other church leaders (v. 9); he spread "malicious nonsense" about the leadership (v. 10); and he interfered with church members who wanted to show welcome to fellow Christians (v. 10).

Perhaps you have had the misfortune of witnessing the disharmony that results when a man or woman seeks to grasp all the honor and attention in a church. These people must always be first—first to give their opinion, first to be consulted, first to be recognized, first to be served, first to be applauded. Building meaningful relationships with such an individual is impossible—to try might even be damaging. People like Diotrephes not only harm the body, they rob themselves of loving, caring relationships.

I wonder if, as he wrote about Diotrephes, John remembered his own failing in this area—the time he and his brother James (with an assist from their mother) asked Jesus for positions of authority in the coming kingdom (Mark 10:35–37).

But it wasn't only these sons of Zebedee—all the disciples angled for their own importance. Who would be the greatest? (Mark 9:34). Even Jesus's disciples sought to be esteemed, honored, respected, and rewarded. They longed to be first. They thought more highly of themselves than they should have. And Jesus always reminded them that the way to greatness was to step back and serve. "Sitting down, Jesus called the Twelve and said, 'Anyone who wants to be first must be the very last, and the servant of all'" (Mark 9:35).

Jesus backed up His words with actions. One time, He had been on a mountainside for days, surrounded by crowds. People were bringing the lame, the blind, and the sick to Him, and He healed them. The people were amazed.

Though Jesus must have been weary from His long, intense ministry, He wasn't done serving. "I have compassion for these people," He said. "They have already been with me three days and have nothing to eat. I do not want to send them away hungry, or they may collapse on the way" (Matthew 15:32). So Jesus fed them—a miraculous meal, starting with seven loaves of bread and a few small fish, that satisfied four thousand men in addition to the women and children present.

Jesus saw people's needs and acted upon them. There could hardly be a more dramatic example than the time He washed His disciples' feet. Jesus was eating His final Passover meal with the Twelve, just before His betrayal and arrest. Suddenly, He got up from the table, wrapped a towel around His waist, and took a bowl of water. Then He knelt before each disciple, washing their feet one by one. This was normally the duty of a household servant, not the King of Kings! But in serving the disciples this way, Jesus showed His love.

When He returned to the table, He explained His actions to the stunned disciples: "Now that I, your Lord and Teacher, have washed your feet, you also should wash one another's feet. I have set you an example that you should do as I have done for you" (John 13:14–15).

Of course, this literal washing of feet was meant to represent any humble, self-sacrificing service to others—visiting a shut-in, providing childcare for a single mom, mentoring a young man in need of a job . . . the possibilities and opportunities are endless. Jesus's selflessness is our example: by putting others first, by honoring and serving us, He showed the way to a healthy and harmonious relationship with the Father.

Harmony and Home

Christian homes should be known by each member's desire to put others first; to show love and honor. Relating to one another with such kindness develops a harmonious and loving family environment.

On Wednesdays, I sometimes babysit two of our grandsons, Aiden and Holden. These four-year-old cousins love being together. They generate more energy than a nuclear power plant. Sometimes, conflict erupts.

Teaching these little guys to share and take turns has been interesting. Sharing requires that one child give preference and honor to another for a time. It is often encouraging to watch their response to the simple statement, "First it is Aiden's turn, then it is Holden's turn." Generally, they agree to this approach, and it is heartwarming to see them willingly hand over a toy or book when their time is up. This is the first step in learning to honor and prefer.

In marriage, honoring and preferring one another can fuel affection and harmony in the relationship. It is so simple: when a husband loads the dishwasher for his tired wife, he is honoring her. When a wife goes out of her way to prepare her husband's favorite recipe, he feels valued.

What works to create harmony in our families is the same as what works in the church: honoring and considering others before ourselves. "Do nothing out of selfish ambition or vain conceit," the apostle Paul wrote. "Rather, in humility value others above yourselves, not looking to your own interests but each of you to the interests of the others" (Philippians 2:3–4).

As we follow Jesus's example of serving and honoring others, putting our spiritual brothers and sisters first, we create a harmonious, affirming church. Who wouldn't feel at home there?

BRINGING IT HOME

- Psalm 133:1 reads, "How good and pleasant it is when God's people live together in unity." When have you experienced the delight of unity in your church family? What was that like?
- Mutual respect, the sharing of a common goal, and careful listening all contributed to the harmony of the Orpheus Orchestra. In which of these areas do you need to grow? How can you more intentionally contribute to a harmonious environment in your church?
- Pride and prejudice, overemphasizing a particular leader, and the inability to compromise all lead to cracks in the

church's foundation. Do you find any of these problems in your own thinking? What can you do to prevent these issues from disrupting the harmony of your church?

- Honor is not flattery, but it is treating others with dignity, respect, and appreciation. Think of a brother or sister you could honor, and find a way to express your esteem.

- To "prefer one another" means to step aside for the benefit of another person. Has anyone ever stepped aside for your sake? How did that impact your relationship? Who might God be calling you to "prefer" today?

- 1 Peter 3:11 says, "Seek peace and pursue it." Make a commitment today to pursue peace and create harmony with your brothers and sisters in Christ.

9

Speak the Truth in Love

Why Truth Matters

It has well been said that truth without love is brutality, but love without truth is hypocrisy.

Warren Wiersbe

Speaking the truth in love, we will grow to become in every respect the mature body of him who is the head, that is, Christ.

Ephesians 4:15

*O*ur four children sat on the orange shag carpet, eyes glued to the TV. It was 1986, and the Space Shuttle *Challenger* was about to launch with a civilian, a school teacher, on board. Just a few months earlier, following a visit to Disney World, we watched from our car as the shuttle left a trail of smoke across the Florida sky. Now, our science-minded kids would witness another launch from their own living room.

The countdown and liftoff happened without a hitch. But as I walked into the kitchen to make lunch, I heard one of the kids ask, "What is that?"

Seventy-three seconds in to the flight, *Challenger* exploded— before the eyes of our children and the whole world. Debris from the shuttle rained down over the Atlantic. On the NASA website, the landing site for that *Challenger* flight is listed as the ocean floor.

Everyone was stunned. Well, nearly everyone. There were a few scientists and technicians who were uncomfortable with a launch in the unusually cold Florida weather. Though they knew the truth of the danger, and tried to share it with launch officials, the determination was made to continue with the flight. Had their concerns been taken seriously, perhaps the members of the *Challenger* crew would be here today with their children and grandchildren.

The truth matters. In some cases, it can be the difference between life and death.

The Apostle Paul Speaks the Truth

There was sin in the Corinthian church. Lots of sin. But one situation particularly concerned Paul. He knew this sin, left unchecked, had the ability to damage the believers' witness and destroy their church. So he wrote them a letter speaking very honestly about the grievous sin—an inappropriate relationship between a man and his own stepmother. If that wasn't bad enough, the church members were "proud"—perhaps of their open-mindedness.

Paul's powerful medicine? "When you are assembled and I am with you in spirit, and the power of our Lord Jesus is present, hand this man over to Satan for the destruction of the flesh, so that his spirit may be saved on the day of the Lord" (1 Corinthians 5:4–5).

The Corinthians' response to Paul's letter could mean the difference between life and death—the life and death of their church.

Some time later, Paul followed up with the Corinthians in a second letter. "Even if I caused you sorrow by my letter, I do not regret it," he wrote. "Though I did regret it—I see that my letter hurt you, but only for a little while—yet now I am happy, not because you were made sorry, but because your sorrow led you to repentance" (2 Corinthians 7:8–9).

The truth won!

Addressing this concern had been difficult and painful. But the outcome saved both the sinning church member and the life of the church. The truth made the difference.

The famed physicist Albert Einstein sought truth in the realm of science, but his comments on the search, as recorded on a statue at the National Academy of Sciences, pertains to our discussion of church: "The right to search for truth implies also a duty; one must not conceal any part of what one has recognized to be true."[34] We have an obligation to speak the truth to each other. When we do, healing and well-being are possible.

When we don't speak truth to our loved ones, though, relationships become unsafe. Imagine a family where parents were afraid or unwilling to tell their children the truth. What if those parents were silent when their son failed to do homework or their daughter spit in the eye of curfews? What if the parents never spoke of the dangers of drug or alcohol abuse?

The safety net that children desperately need would have gaping holes in it. Those teens or young adults might have the freedom they want, but not the protection they need. They would grow to resent their parents for the lack of guidance.

It takes a great deal of maturity to speak the truth in love. Truth matters. Truth is any family's safety net.

Speak the Truth in Love, and Grow Up

In Ephesians 4, Paul describes the believers' unity. We are joined together by "one Lord, one faith, one baptism" (v. 5). With this in mind, he instructs us to deal with one another with both love and truth. The life we share together is too precious, and came at too high a cost, to corrupt with dishonesty. Truth matters. So does love.

Paul describes a church filled with God-given leaders—apostles, prophets, evangelists, pastors, and teachers—who "equip" others to build up the body and reach unity in their faith (vv. 11–12). "Then we will no longer be infants," Paul wrote, "tossed back and forth by the waves, and blown here and there by every wind of teaching and by the cunning and craftiness of people in their deceitful scheming" (v. 14)

Children are easily deceived. And, as is also true with adults, they often run from the truth. Paul was calling the Ephesian church to put away their childish inclinations and move toward Christian maturity. A big part of that is truth: "Instead, speaking the truth in love," he wrote, "we will grow to become in every respect the mature body of him who is the head, that is, Christ" (Ephesians 4:15).

I once worked in a women's ministry office, where I became friends with Marilyn, a Christian counselor. Her job was to help churches handle conflict. We lovingly dubbed Marilyn the Director of Church Conflict, though she preferred to be known as the Director of Church Health.

Marilyn's job was stressful but she was undaunted. She offered the churches tools to help them walk through their conflict. Her counsel led many congregations to more meaningful relationships and ministries.

Church conflict is complex. But one thing I learned from Marilyn was this: Most of the issues she encountered were the result of leadership's failure in this area of speaking the truth in love. Either the leaders didn't speak the truth and deal with problems in a healthy, constructive way, or they spoke the truth without love and did irreparable damage to one another.

Marilyn's wise observations? "If you can't speak the truth in love, don't speak at all. If you don't love someone enough to speak the truth, you have a bigger problem."

Truth Is Dangerous

Speak the truth? That feels threatening. And who am I to point out truth to another believer? I certainly have issues of my own. Doesn't that let me off the hook?

Not according to Jesus. "How can you say to your brother," the Lord said, "'Let me take the speck out of your eye,' when you yourself fail to see the plank in your own eye? You hypocrite, first take the plank out of your eye, and then you will see clearly to remove the speck from your brother's eye" (Luke 6:42).

Jesus never told us to ignore our fellow believers' sins. He simply said to address our own sin first. Then, and only then, can we help our brothers and sisters. We have an obligation to be honest with ourselves as well as with our spiritual siblings.

The Victorian Christian novelist and poet George MacDonald said it well. "Friends, if we be honest with ourselves, we shall be honest with each other." When we are honest—with God, with ourselves, and with other believers—we create a safe church where each brother and sister can "grow up."

When We Don't Speak the Truth in Love

When we fear speaking the truth in love, some of us stumble into passive-aggressive behavior. We don't want to say what needs to be said. We prefer sending subtle, negative messages—a cold shoulder, a withering glance, a sigh. We hope the intended recipient will read our minds. But if they don't pick up the cues, we might forsake our passive ways for more aggressive behavior.

The not-so-simple remedy for our passive-aggressive behavior is speaking the truth in love. We need courage. Yes, speaking the truth is risky. We may offend and temporarily (or permanently) lose a relationship. However, when we identify the other person's welfare as our highest goal, we find the courage to say what must be said.

When we lovingly express our own thoughts, feelings, and opinions to our brothers and sisters, they come to know who we are and what we value. Our appreciation for one another grows.

By contrast, some believers are all about truth telling. In fact, they are brutal in their honesty. They have a passion to set other people straight. They can serve an important function in the body, but they struggle with giving grace and showing love. The remedy for this kind of brutal honesty is a realization of and gratitude for the grace and mercy God extends to everyone.

When we bring truth and love together in what we say, we follow the example of Jesus. As the apostle John said, "For the law was given through Moses; grace and truth came through Jesus Christ" (John 1:17).

Reflect for a moment on Jesus's interactions with people:

With "the woman at the well," Jesus lovingly offered the living water. Then He gently spoke the truth regarding her sin: "The fact is, you have had five husbands, and the man you now have is not your husband" (John 4:18).

To a woman caught in adultery, Jesus expressed love and grace. After dismissing the angry crowd who'd brought the woman to Him, by suggesting that any of them without sin should be the first to throw stones at her, He said to the woman, "Neither do I condemn you" (John 8:11). Then He sent her on her way with truth: she needed to leave her life of sin.

In the dark of night, Jesus made time for Nicodemus. Though he wasn't as proud and antagonistic as his fellow Pharisees, Nicodemus needed the truth that Jesus spoke to him: "No one can see the kingdom of God unless they are born again" (John 3:3). But Jesus didn't end the conversation there—He went on to explain exactly how to be born again: "For God so loved the world that he gave his one and only Son, that whoever believes in him shall not perish but have eternal life" (John 3:16).

The apostle John says Jesus is "full of grace and truth" (John 1:14). Jesus is our example. Though we will never achieve His perfect balance of speaking the truth in love, we have a lifetime to work on it.

The Tightrope of Truth and Love

I've only been to one circus. Looking up to watch the tightrope walkers made me dizzy. I could hardly watch! I hated the thought of that lovely lady in the pink leotard plummeting to the ground.

Circus performers can fall off either side of a tightrope. Whether it's the right or the left doesn't matter. They will hit the ground either way—unless there is a net.

The same is true of speaking the truth in love. We can fall off the side of love. Or we can fall off the side of truth. Either way, there is danger.

With brutal, uncaring honesty we can damage our relationships as well as our credibility. If we earn a reputation as someone who angrily confronts others, our fellow believes may shy away. Can they trust us with their problems? In the same way, to refuse to speak the truth a brother or sister needs to hear is equally risky. Under the guise of love, we can let them walk into danger. When we refuse to speak the truth in love, we are putting our own comfort ahead of our brother or sister's well-being.

We count on our spiritual family to speak the truth to us in loving ways. When we are confident that we can trust our fellow believers, knowing they will kindly and gently speak truth to us, we feel safe and at ease. Our church becomes our safety net.

What we need is balance, the grace and the truth of Jesus. We can ask for His help to walk the tightrope with poise and steadiness. When we've learned to maintain this delicate balance, we have nothing to fear from our brothers and sisters.

I frequently speak with people who have unaddressed relational issues. Often, I will gently suggest, "Why don't you try speaking the truth in love?" Many times, they get a look of terror on their faces, proclaiming, "Oh, I could never do that. I hate confrontation."

But that is a myth! Speaking the truth in love does not equal confrontation. In fact, speaking the truth in love is just the opposite. Confrontation is argumentative and results in winners and losers. It's like a political debate. That doesn't sound very loving, does it?

When we confront someone, our goal is to convince the other person to come over to our way of thinking. We are generally seeking victory. Sometimes we are simply so angry, hurt, or frustrated that we just want to speak our mind.

But when we speak the truth in love, we speak from concern. We want what is best for the other person. We desire health for the entire body of Christ. We put the spiritual interests of a fellow believer above our own.

Speaking the truth in love is a sign of maturity. It takes spiritual courage to do what is best for our brother or sister. We are willing to tolerate the discomfort and risk of speaking the truth because we love others.

It is a way of building people up. "Speaking the truth in love, we will grow to become in every respect the mature body of him who is the head, that is, Christ. From him the whole body, joined and held together by every supporting ligament, grows and builds itself up in love, as each part does its work" (Ephesians 4:15–16).

So how do we speak the truth in love without being confrontational? Wait. Take time to pray and seek God's guidance. Don't rush into a difficult conversation unprepared. Seek counsel from a godly friend if you need direction. Deal with your own anger first. Take to heart Jesus's admonition to remove the plank from your own eye before pointing out the speck in another's eye. Immerse yourself in God's Word—it never fails to instruct us. Gather up your courage. Speaking the truth in love can be risky and frightening. Remind yourself that the spiritual welfare of a brother or sister is at stake and is worth the risk. Then just do it.

And be sure to remember the wisdom of Proverbs 15:1—"A gentle answer turns away wrath, but a harsh word stirs up anger."

Hearing Truth

As hard as it is to speak the truth in love, hearing the truth is even more difficult. When a brother or sister takes us aside to point out our blind spots, we often feel criticized, misunderstood, foolish, or vulnerable. Nothing exhibits our Christian maturity better than a willingness to hear hard truth from another believer.

Is it possible to *receive* the truth with grace and gratitude? Of course. The key is inviting others to participate in our spiritual growth. When we give others the permission to speak the truth in love to us, we can receive their correction with humility and appreciation. When we actually welcome input from other brothers and sisters, we contribute to a safe environment where we can help one another to grow.

Since we have been working on this book, Ray has suffered a minor stroke. Our first reaction was shock: How could a healthy, active sixty-four year old with good blood pressure and cholesterol have a stroke? Our second reaction was gratitude: the stroke's effects were limited mainly to Ray's visual cortex. He now has an actual "blind spot" that will affect him every day.

To help manage this condition, Ray has invited me to point out what is in his blind spot. "Watch out, there is a person with a grocery cart coming from your left. . . . Look out for the little kids running through the foyer. . . . Careful, your elbow is dangerously close to that glass of iced tea!"

We all have blind spots, whether physical or spiritual. From time to time, we all need someone to help us see what we are missing so we can avoid danger. When we speak the truth in love and invite others to speak the truth into our own lives, we create a safe environment for every member of the family.

Gossip Is Never Truthful or Loving

Gossip is harmless enough, right?

The apostle Paul didn't think so. Gossip is so destructive that Paul included it in a list of sins that characterize people who reject the knowledge of God: "They have become filled with every kind of wickedness, evil, greed and depravity. They are full of envy, murder, strife, deceit and malice. They are gossips, slanderers, God-haters, insolent, arrogant and boastful; they invent ways of doing evil" (Romans 1:29–30). Just as we as followers of Jesus want to distance ourselves from the sins of greed and strife, we must grasp the seriousness of the sin of gossip. Gossip causes pain. Gossip ruins reputations. Gossip separates friends. Gossip destroys churches and families. Gossip weakens our witness. Haven't we all watched in dismay as gossip has done its devastating work?

According to Merriam-Webster, a gossip is someone who discloses "information about the behavior and personal lives of other people." Whenever we share the personal and private matters of another person, we are gossiping. We have no right to share a brother or sister's personal story or struggle. Their story belongs only to them.

In Leviticus 19:16, God himself warned the Israelites not to "go about spreading slander among your people." According to Bible commentator John Gill, the picture here is of a peddler going from place to place to sell his wares. This visual is similar to the warnings given in 1 Timothy 5:13, where the apostle Paul cautioned young widows against being busybodies, going from house to house to discuss things that were none of their business.

Gossip should have no place in the life of a believer. So what do we do when we are tempted to join in? First, we ask God for wisdom. James 3 reminds us of how dangerous and harmful our speech can be to others. But, James continues, "the wisdom that comes from heaven is first of all pure; then peace-loving, considerate, submissive, full of mercy and good fruit, impartial and sincere. Peacemakers who sow in peace reap a harvest of righteousness" (James 3:17–18). Second, we commit ourselves to never sharing the personal and private matters of another person. We choose to mind our own business—and if gossip bubbles up in a conversation, we remind our brothers and sisters to respect our fellow believer's privacy. Third, if we have true concern about a person, we go directly to that person and offer our prayers and support.

When you slice into the tough, green rind of a watermelon, what do you suppose you will find? Of course, you assume you will see deep red fruit dotted with smooth, black seeds—not the creamy white fruit of a banana. When we call ourselves Christians, the world has an expectation of us: that we will not only look and sound like Christians, but that we will *act* like Christians, loving our fellow believers from the heart. This love should color the way we speak to and about other believers. Our outside appearance—our profession of faith—should indicate to others what is on our inside, namely a sincere love for God's people.

Committing ourselves to honesty and integrity toward one another creates a safe and loving environment in the church. We can share our concerns and worries without fear of having our privacy violated. When we know we are safe from unkind words and hurtful gossip we feel at home.

Quick to Listen, Slow to Speak

"My dear brothers and sisters, take note of this," the Bible writer James said. "Everyone should be quick to listen, slow to speak and slow to become angry" (James 1:19). This verse reminds me of a humorous experience I had in France.

Five o'clock was dinnertime for our family, but shortly after our arrival in Menton, we heard a strange sound from the apartment above. At 9:30 each evening we heard loud footsteps and the scraping of chairs. This went on until a little after ten. Just as we were putting on our pajamas, our upstairs neighbors seemed to be having a party. Actually, we learned they were having dinner.

You might wonder how French children make it from lunch time until this late dinner hour. The answer is *aperitif.*

Aperitif is a European custom. Some think of it as a cocktail hour, but for most French it is not—it is a time for light snacks with friends. Many French people are more comfortable inviting guests for aperitif than for a late dinner.

On Friday evenings, we walked down Avenue Nationale to the home of our friends Eve and Michel. An aperitif featuring cheese, crackers, nuts, hard boiled quail's eggs dipped in ketchup, and a variety of juices or sparkling waters was set out on one of Eve's beautiful tablecloths. It was a time of good snacks and good conversation.

After some time, I finally found the courage to host aperitif myself. I re-created Eve's menu with one addition: *porcs dans une couverture* or—as we know them—pigs in a blanket. Eve and Michel's children loved them. Of course, she wanted the recipe.

In broken French, I rattled off the ingredients and instructions on how to make the finger food so foreign to our French friends. Eve smiled.

It wasn't until she left that I realized that in my feeble French I had told her to bake them until midnight. I should have instructed her to bake them for ten minutes.

Perhaps I should have been "slow to speak."

Our time in France taught me the importance of listening carefully and not speaking in haste. Since French was difficult for me, I had no choice but to listen carefully. By paying close attention, I learned things I never could have while talking.

Most of us struggle with truly listening to others. Like many people, I am always considering how I want to respond, what I want to say next. I frequently remind myself that I need to listen more than I speak. A humorous reminder attributed to Mark Twain helps: "If we were supposed to talk more than we listen, we would have two tongues and one ear."

If we want our brothers and sisters to feel at home in the church, we need to learn to listen—and listen well. When we truly hear the concerns of others, they feel loved. As author and professor David Augsburger has written, "Being heard is so close to being loved that for the average person, they are almost indistinguishable."[35]

One secret to listening is making friends with silence. Too often, we mistake talking for communication. But it is when we listen in silence that true communication takes place.

People who come to my office are sometimes unnerved when I am silent for a long time. They are not accustomed to someone actually listening to them. But they like it. They come back for more.

In the psalms, David prayed, "Incline your ear, O Lord, and answer me" (Psalm 86:1 ESV). This picture, of God bending down to hear us, reminds me of home. When our little grandchildren come to visit, I often stoop down to their level to hear their requests. I can miss five-year-old Madelyn's soft voice if I don't incline, or lean, my ear toward her. I want to hear Madelyn. We all need to hear each other.

Speak the Truth . . . in Song

Music is powerful. It soothes. It encourages. It comforts. It reminds us of our beliefs and heritage. It teaches truth. It creates an environment of celebration and community. The Christian's heritage of music is part of our identity and should be treasured.

This year, after an important decision in our nation's capital, our church's worship leader started the congregation on the great hymn by Martin Luther, "A Mighty Fortress Is Our God." After the first line, so that the entire focus would be on God, he walked off the platform. With no musicians before us, we as a church sang to our mighty God and to one another. During those few moments, we encouraged each other's faith in a time of discouragement. We proclaimed our beliefs as a body through song. We were one.

It was a glimpse of heaven, and at that moment, I felt more at home in our church than ever before.

Music is a powerful gift to the church. We sing to glorify God, and we sing to encourage one another. "Be filled with the Spirit," the apostle Paul wrote, "speaking to one another with psalms, hymns, and songs from the Spirit. Sing and make music in your heart to the Lord" (Ephesians 5:18–19).

What kind of music? All kinds. Psalms, hymns, and spiritual songs. The main requirements are that they be theologically correct, directed to God and come from sincere hearts.

We may not always think of music as a way of teaching, but that's exactly how Colossians 3:16 describes it: "Let the message of Christ dwell among you richly as you teach and admonish one another with all wisdom through psalms, hymns, and songs from the Spirit, singing to God with gratitude in your hearts."

This verse implies that, through our music, we share Christian truth again and again. The lyrics of this music would instruct, inspire, and encourage. It would clearly identify us as believers who share a common faith. It should also reflect the diversity of who we are as members of the body of Christ.

When my children were small, I sang to them. No one was completely tucked in until we all sang "Jesus Loves Me" and "Away in a Manger." We also made up songs that were just for our family—I rubbed many a toddler's back while singing my own creation, "My Chickadee, My Chickadee, I Love My Little Chickadee." Those songs became part of our identity as parents and children. Now, I sing the songs to my grandkids.

The music we sang soothed and comforted our small children, teaching them about Jesus and reminding them that they were loved. The music we sing in church can soothe and comfort our spiritual siblings, teaching us all about God and reminding us that we are part of a larger family. It is an important part of helping people feel at home.

Truth Brings Us Home

To the church in Colosse, the apostle Paul had written, "Let the message of Christ dwell among you richly as you teach and admonish one another with all wisdom through psalms, hymns, and songs from the spirit, singing to God with gratitude in your hearts" (Colossians 3:16). In this church, which met in the home of a man named Philemon, we see an example of the power of communicating the truth in love. It could even bring freedom to a runaway slave.

Philemon was apparently a wealthy citizen of Colosse. He had a home big enough to host the city's Christian church, and he owned at least one slave. Philemon had come to faith in Jesus Christ through Paul's influence, and what we now know as "the book of Philemon" was a personal letter from Paul to his spiritual son.

Paul began by expressing love and appreciation for Philemon and his faithful service to the church in Colosse. He remembered how often Philemon's ministry had refreshed God's people. Then, choosing his words carefully, Paul gently and humbly spoke truth to a difficult situation.

Philemon's slave, Onesimus, had run away to Rome, where he came into contact with Paul. Onesimus may have even stolen from his master before his flight. How would Paul know that? Perhaps Onesimus had confessed to him.

From his imprisonment in Rome, Paul told Philemon that his runaway slave had heard the truth of the gospel and ministered to Paul's needs. While the slave's absence may have been an aggravation to his master, Paul said Philemon would ultimately benefit from it. "Perhaps the reason he was separated from you for a little while was that you might have him back forever—no longer as a slave, but better than a slave, as a dear brother" (vv. 15–16).

The name Onesimus means "useful," but Paul acknowledged that had had become "useless" to Philemon. Happily, those useless days were now over. Transformed by the truth, his value was no longer in fulfilling the duties of a household slave. Onesimus had a higher calling: he was Paul's helper in spreading the gospel. "Formerly he was useless to you, but now he has become useful both to you and to me" (v. 11).

Speaking the truth in love to our Christian family requires sensitivity, humility, gentleness, and courage. A willingness to lovingly say what needs to be said is a sign of our commitment to the health of the family of God. It builds our church home here on earth . . . and prepares us for our eternal home with all believers of all time.

BRINGING IT HOME

- What is your greatest fear about speaking the truth in love? How could speaking the truth in love benefit people in your life?

- Are you more of a truth-teller or a grace-giver? How does your particular style complicate speaking the truth in love? Have you confused confrontation with speaking the truth in love? If so, review the differences discussed earlier in this chapter.

- How have you seen gossip negatively impact your church? What about flattery? What do people need to know to overcome this tendency?

- Are you quick to listen? How can you cultivate this skill? Who in your church needs your listening ear?

- What role does music play in your relationship with other believers?

10

Members of His Household

Homesick No More

Consequently, you are no longer foreigners and strangers, but fellow citizens with God's people and also members of his household.

Ephesians 2:19

All of my family had relocated to other parts of the country—or to heaven. Still, I convinced Ray of my need to visit my hometown in Ohio. I yearned to reconnect with my roots. For me, it was a mission to see my grandmother's house one last time.

I imagined stepping onto the front porch where my sisters and I had played house. Would the swing still serenade me with its familiar squeak? Could I sit where we sat for hours with our grandmother, watching sunsets? Maybe I would peek through the windows of the sunroom that once held Grandma's cacti and the credenza filled with a collection of glass elephants. I would point out to Ray the corner of the sunroom where a wooden radio console had reigned for decades.

And our visit would be incomplete without seeing Aunt Nettie's house. In my childhood, my great aunt's neat and tidy home radiated curb appeal. A covered front porch ran the length of the white house. The wooden porch floor, painted shiny green, was adorned with a straw welcome mat. Peonies and hydrangeas circled the yard. Aunt Nettie's house was worthy of the cover of *Southern Living* magazine.

But I was in for a shock. When we reached the old neighborhood, I couldn't believe my eyes. A business now occupied Grandmother's home. No swing was on the front porch. New siding and a cheap brick façade made the house nearly unrecognizable. The wood framed windows, which Grandmother always polished to a shining gleam with vinegar and water, now looked dark and dirty. The concrete driveway, poured one wheelbarrow at a time by my handyman grandfather, had cracked and buckled. No sign remained of the little girls' names that Grandpa had written in the cement with a whittled stick. Asphalt covered what was once a lush front yard. The entire residence had the look of disrepair.

The condition of Aunt Nettie's house might have been even more depressing. No peony bushes. No hydrangeas. Maple trees gone. And who cut down the cherry tree? Paper and broken toys littered the garden plots where flowers should have been. A rusty motorcycle, as dilapidated as the house, rested carelessly on its side in the middle of the lawn. The peeling paint, sagging front steps, and cracked windows sent a message that the current residents did not appreciate the potential of this once graceful home.

Our thirty-minute slog down memory lane gave new meaning to the term *homesick*. A sense of loss and grief swept over me as we returned to our car. My hopes of connecting with sweet memories of laughter and love crumbled as surely as the old houses had. Everything that had once said "home" to me was gone. I felt empty and abandoned.

We got in the car to return to our Illinois home. Soon, as we navigated the twists and turns of a country highway, I began to realize what was bothering me so much. It wasn't the houses or the gardens or the porch swing I was missing.

I was homesick for the people I had loved, homesick for the people who had loved me.

I missed their laughter.

I missed the hospitality they shared when making chicken and dumplings or hosting birthday parties.

I missed the words of support spoken before a choir concert or a challenging math test.

I missed the moments of comfort and affection when life was disappointing and scary.

I missed the gentle words and songs about God and His love and the beauty of His creation.

I missed the TLC when strep throat or a stomach virus meant a day off from school.

I missed the stories that gave my life a sense of history and taught me important life lessons.

I missed the gift of books for each birthday and Christmas, and the pep talk on the importance of education that came with them.

I missed the honest truth spoken in love that kept me from dangerous detours in life.

I missed the unconditional acceptance and love that made my relatives' house a home.

When I had imagined stepping onto my grandmother's front porch, what I really longed for was Grandma herself. I wanted her to swing open the wooden screen door and say, "Welcome home. Come on in. I'll make you a cup of tea."

Aren't we all a little homesick? Doesn't everyone long for a permanent place where we can be loved, accepted, cared for, mentored, encouraged, and shown hospitality? A place where the door swings wide open and we are welcomed without end? A place where we are cherished by gentle friends and our loneliness is banished?

I believe we hear a hint of this when the writer of Ecclesiastes says God has "set eternity in the human heart" (3:11). We have an intense longing for our heavenly home, for the beauty of an eternal family.

Until the day we settle into our final home and receive what C. S. Lewis called "the healing of that old ache,"[36] God has given us the church as a refuge. Loving each other, caring for one another, we create a relational environment that comforts and soothes our wistful, homesick hearts.

A Forever Home and Eternal Family

The earthly church is a spiritual family that foreshadows the true, heavenly community for which our hearts long. For the believer, filled with the Holy Spirit, homesickness for a heavenly home only increases with each passing year. Awaiting us, just over the horizon, are the life and relationships for which we were made. Our hearts tell us this is true. Our belief in this future home fills us with hope.

The apostle Paul knew well the pain of homesickness. He ached, groaned, agonized over, waited for, thirsted, and hungered for his heavenly dwelling. "We know that if the earthly tent we live in is destroyed, we have a building from God, an eternal house in heaven, not built by human hands," he wrote to believers in Corinth. "Meanwhile we groan, longing to be clothed instead with our heavenly dwelling, because when we are clothed, we will not be found naked. For while we are in this tent, we groan and are burdened, because we do not wish to be unclothed but to be clothed instead with our heavenly dwelling, so that what is mortal may be swallowed up by life" (2 Corinthians 5:1–4).

Paul knew that his world—what we could call the first-century Middle East—was not his true home. Even his Roman citizenship, so valued by people of Paul's time and place, really counted for nothing. With spiritual passport in hand, he longed for the day when he would get his visa and could fully participate in his birthright as a Christian believer. "Our citizenship is in heaven," he wrote. "And we eagerly await a Savior from there, the Lord Jesus Christ" (Philippians 3:20).

The psalm writer David reminds us that our next home will be an enduring one. "I will dwell in the house of the LORD forever" (Psalm 23:6). David longed for that time as much as the apostle Paul did. "One thing I ask from the LORD," David wrote, "this only do I seek: that I may dwell in the house of the LORD all the days of my life, to gaze on the beauty of the LORD and to seek him in his temple" (Psalm 27:4).

David anticipated the joy of seeing his Savior's beauty. This is the most thrilling and important aspect of our eternal home: we will be with our heavenly Father forever. Our worship and relationship with Him will take on new dimensions as we are able to live in the complete awareness of His presence.

On the days when we are blessed to have an eternal perspective, we recognize that our time on earth is short. At best, our citizenship here is temporary and flawed. The houses we call home will crumble. The loved ones we cherish today will soon be gone. With these realities in mind, we look forward to a permanent residence—a heavenly home.

There, God himself will put an end to our homesickness and loneliness. "Look, God's home is now among his people! He will live with them, and they will be his people. God himself will be with them" (Revelation 21:3 NLT). But until that time, God has given us a preview.

The church on earth is a foreshadowing of God's great goal: to create a united, like-minded people made up of every tribe and nation who will worship before His throne. This is why we obey Jesus's command in Matthew 28:19–20: "Therefore go and make disciples of all nations, baptizing them in the name of the Father and of the Son and of the Holy Spirit, and teaching them to obey everything I have commanded you."

One glorious day, free from geographic boundaries and the limitations of time zones, emancipated from all prejudice and bias, we will gather from the four corners of the earth. The church, with Jesus as its head, will stand as a complete body before God. Here is how John described that day, in the book of Revelation: "I looked, and there before me was a great multitude that no one could count, from every nation, tribe, people and language, standing before the throne and before the Lamb. They were wearing white robes and were holding palm branches in their hands. And they cried out in a loud voice: 'Salvation belongs to our God, who sits on the throne, and to the Lamb'" (Revelation 7:9–10).

Consider this multitude of believers assembled before God's throne. I believe that, suddenly, the importance of our earthly relationships, our shared faith, our corporate worship, and our prayers for one another will hit us full force. In this great company of saints, we will look into each other's eyes with gratitude as we realize we had shared the joys and sorrows of life on the journey to this very place and time. We will clasp our fellow worshippers' hands, understanding that we had been in the company of saints all along.

The Great Reunion

We will hold citizenship in a heavenly city. God will make His home among us. He will heal the ache and loneliness. We will freely worship alongside believers from every nation.

But what about our loved ones? Will we be reunited with our own families? What about the people with whom we've worshipped, the Christian brothers and sisters we loved, forgave, accepted, and comforted? Those for whom we prayed? Will they be part of our forever family? Will our longing for them ever end?

The first-century Thessalonians had questions like that. They were worried and anxious. They anticipated Christ's return, but what about their family members and fellow Christians who were already dead and buried? What would happen to them?

The apostle Paul offered comfort:

> Brothers and sisters, we do not want you to be uninformed about those who sleep in death, so that you do not grieve like the rest of mankind, who have no hope. For we believe that Jesus died and rose again, and so we believe that God will bring with Jesus those who have fallen asleep in him. According to the Lord's word, we tell you that we who are still alive, who are left until the coming of the Lord, will certainly not precede those who have fallen asleep. For the Lord himself will come down from heaven, with a loud command, with the voice of the archangel and with the trumpet call of God, and the dead in Christ will rise first. After that, we who are still alive and are left will be caught up together with them in the clouds to meet the Lord in the air. And so we will be with the Lord forever. Therefore encourage one another with these words.
>
> 1 Thessalonians 4:13–18

Christians will be together forever. Our earthly relationships have an eternal dimension: the bonds we have nurtured in this life—with our heavenly Father, with our brothers and sisters in Christ, and with believing members of our own families—will never break. We will continue and deepen these loving connections throughout eternity.

The moment we step into heaven, all homesickness will end. Our loneliness will evaporate. The ache and longing will be gone. I expect my grandmother to swing open the door and say, "Welcome home. Come on in. I'll make you a cup of tea."

Pastor and author Max Lucado describes our homecoming reunion like this:

> Just as a returning soldier drops his duffel when he sees his wife, you'll drop your longing when you see your Father. Those you love will shout. Those you know will applaud. But all the noise will cease when he cups your chin and says, "Welcome home."[37]

The Apologetic of Love

People in our neighborhoods, cities, and towns are as homesick as we are—though in many cases, they don't realize what they're longing for.

It's been said that every human being has a "God-shaped vacuum" in their soul. Ideally, the church should help them to fill it. Some might respect the church enough as an institution to wonder if our particular congregation is a place they could find a taste of heaven. Others may never give our churches a thought—or worse, might feel antagonistic toward the faith in general and our body in particular.

Perhaps the question we need to ask ourselves, in our own Christian communities, is this: do the love and care we show one another demonstrate the love of Christ to the world? Does our ability to forgive, empathize, accept, and encourage one another attract non-believers to Christianity? Does our love give the world a glimpse of our heavenly home?

Recently, Ray and I have visited three very different churches, all within an hour's drive of our home. The first, in a northern Chicago suburb, initially attracted us by the beauty of its facility. As we entered the sanctuary, we were quietly greeted by a few members. We were moved by the reverence of the people and the simplicity of the surroundings. Musicians were seated off to the side, not on the platform; there was no dominant personality and no showmanship. Clearly, the musicians were there to serve the congregation by using their gifts to the glory of God. The message on discipleship encouraged listeners to closely follow Jesus. It was obvious Ray and I were on the same page with our brothers and sisters in this church—as we drove home, I remarked, "I could make myself at home here."

Rural Wisconsin was home to the second church. We were greeted warmly by more than a few people as we made our way to seats. We watched as person after person greeted the pastor; he returned each greeting with a smile, a hearty handshake, and often some chitchat or laughter. The love between pastor and people was obvious. A strong biblical message was followed by the baptism of three young men, all in their teens. Dozens of family and friends clustered around the baptistery to watch these boys take an important step in their spiritual journey. The warmth and love Ray and I saw caused us both to brush away a tear. Leaving this church, it was Ray's turn to say, "I could make myself at home there."

In the third church, Ray served as pulpit supply. It was a nearby congregation, and a couple of its members are long-time friends. From them, I have heard of the support and care that these believers give one another. Some of them have been part of this church for more than fifty years. They have certainly made themselves at home. Being with this spiritual family was a joyous experience for us—and yes, we could make ourselves at home here too.

I mentioned earlier in this book that Francis Schaeffer, the great theologian and writer, said the most compelling apologetic for the Christian faith is "the observable love of true Christians for true Christians."

As members of our own neighborhoods and communities see our churches, are we displaying the love of Jesus in the way we treat one other? It is critical that we earn a reputation as loving, caring, encouraging, merciful, and hospitable people. If that is truly who we are, the homesick and lonely will be attracted to our churches, finding a place to make themselves at home. The hurting and rejected will find hope and healing.

As we swing open the doors to our churches, others will hear what their hearts long for: "Welcome home."

Rehabbing Our Home

My grandmother's home had deteriorated because of neglect. The beauty of my aunt's home had faded because no one cared. Not one person was willing to invest their time, money, or talents to keep these once-appealing homes nice. In their current condition, it would be impossible for me ever again to feel at home in them. And few if any buyers would be eager to choose these houses for their own families.

Each of them requires work—an incredible amount of repair and tender loving care. Both cry out for someone to see their hidden potential, to be willing to make the sacrifices needed to restore them to beauty.

But cosmetic changes won't be enough. These houses need to comply with codes and regulations. Perhaps even structural repairs are needed to give them strength and insure safety for future tenants.

The love, care, and stewardship of a home is a lot of work.

The same is true of our human relationships. The love, care, and stewardship of our God-ordained spiritual family takes effort. But we dare not neglect the heart of the church.

Some of our connections in the church scream for a serious rehab. At other times, they just need a bit of skillful repair. But they always need diligent maintenance. Updating our programs or changing our presentation to attract new members may not be enough to solve the struggles of our churches. Such surface fixes rarely get to the heart of our pain. No, some serious relational work is in order if our goal is to make our churches the kind of place where everyone feels at home.

But we're not left to guess at solutions. God has a plan for our church relationships—He's given us the "one another" commands to guide us in creating a loving and caring atmosphere for our spiritual family.

The "one another" commands are just that—commands. They are not suggestions. They are directives that help us move toward God's standard for our relationships. As we embrace the "one another" commands, our church family will grow stronger. There will be security and emotional safety.

Our heavenly Father sees the potential for loving relationships in the church. He knows the beauty we'll find as we love and care for one another. He created the relationship between believers in the church to be a powerful witness to the reality of Jesus Christ. With His help, we can become a church that radiates Christ's love to the world.

The night Jesus was betrayed, He issued a clarion call to believers: "A new command I give you: Love one another. As I have loved you, so you must love one another" (John 13:34). Notice that the command was not to "be loved," but to love. If we spend our days looking for the perfect church—a church where we will always be loved and accepted by our fellow Christians—we will probably be disappointed. But if we seek a church where we can love and serve others in Jesus's name, we will never be disappointed.

We can love others because we are already loved by Jesus. The love, acceptance, welcome, hospitality, forgiveness, kindness, and encouragement that we long for can be found in abundance in our relationship with Christ. Because He has shown us love, acceptance, welcome, hospitality, forgiveness, kindness, and encouragement, we—with full and grateful hearts—can do the same for one another. We can put down roots at church and commit ourselves to the lifelong process of making ourselves at home with our spiritual family.

Your Christian brothers and sisters are here for loving on. Tenderly care for the heart of your church so that it will become a place of encouragement, kindness, forgiveness, generosity, and mutual support, a place where you and many others can make yourselves at home.

Notes

Chapter 1: Members One of Another

1. Cloud-Townsend Resources. "Dependency—Key to Our Needs" by John Townsend, July 26, 2000, http://www.cloudtownsend.com /dependency-key-to-our-needs-view-printable-version/

2. Hidden Brain: A Conversation about Life's Unseen Patterns. "The Key to Disaster Survival? Friends and Neighbors," last modified July 21, 2011, http://www .npr.org/templates/transcript/transcript.php?storyId=137526401

3. Ibid.

4. Frontline. "The Great Appeal: What Did Christianity Offer Its Believers That Made It Worth Social Estrangement, Hostility from Neighbors, and Possible Persecution?" April 1998. http://www.pbs.org/wgbh/pages/frontline/shows /religion/why/appeal.html

Chapter 2: Love One Another

5. Francis Schaeffer, *The Mark of the Christian* (Downers Grove, IL: Intervarsity Press, 1970), 29.

6. Bible.org, quoting J. I. Packer, *Your Father Loves You* (Wheaton, IL: Harold Shaw Publishers, 1986), March 10 entry. http://bible.org/illustration/agape-love

7. Andrew Rankin, *Do Love: A Love Hack's Path to Spiritual Maturity* (Bloomington, IN: WestBow Press, 2013), 125.

8. C. S. Lewis, *God in the Dock* (Grand Rapids, MI: Wm. B. Eerdmans Publishing Company, 2014), 35.

9. Barna. "What Millennials Want When They Visit Church." March 4, 2015. https://www.barna.org/barna-update/millennials/711-what-millennials-want -when-they-visit-church#.Vo7UwvkrKM8

Chapter 3: Greet and Accept One Another

10. Corrie ten Boom, *The Hiding Place* (Grand Rapids, MI: Chosen Books, 2006), pg. 69.
11. Dorothy Bass, *Receiving the Day* (San Francisco: Jossey-Bass, Inc., 2000), 117.
12. Christine D. Pohl, *Making Room: Recovering Hospitality as a Christian Tradition* (Grand Rapids, MI: Wm. B. Eerdmans, 1999), 172.
13. Gary Thomas, *Sacred Marriage* (Grand Rapids, MI: Zondervan, 2015), 16.

Chapter 4: Bear One Another's Burdens

14. Henri Nouwen, *Out of Solitude: Three Meditations for the Christian Life* (Notre Dame, IN: Ave Maria Press, 2004), 38.
15. Merriam Webster Online. "Forbearance," http://www.merriam-webster. com/dictionary/forbearance
16. The Globe and Mail. "Thatcherisms: 'If you want something said, ask a man; if you want something done, ask a woman'" by Ann Hui, April 8, 2013, http://www.theglobeandmail.com/news/world/thatcherisms-if-you-want -something-said-ask-a-man-if-you-want-something-done-ask-a-woman/ article10841341/

Chapter 5: Encourage, Build Up, Be Kind to, and Forgive One Another

17. Henry Cloud, *Integrity: The Courage to Meet the Demands of Reality* (New York: HarperCollins Publishers, 2006), 91.
18. The Churchill Centre. "Be Ye Men of Valor," accessed March 29, 2016, http://www.winstonchurchill.org/resources/speeches/233-1940-the-finest-hour /91-be-ye-men-of-valour.
19. YourDictionary.com. "Mellow," http://www.yourdictionary.com/mellow.
20. John Gottman, *The Seven Principles for Making Marriage Work* (New York: Harmony Books, 2015), 25.
21. Max Lucado, *When God Whispers Your Name* (Nashville: Thomas Nelson, 2009), 70.
22. William Eleazar Barton, *The Life of Clara Barton: Founder of the American Red Cross, Volume 2* (Boston: Houghton-Mifflin Company, 1922), 345.
23. Anne Lamott, *Plan B: Further Thoughts on Faith* (New York: Riverhead Books, 2005), 47.

Chapter 7: Confess Your Sins and Pray for Each Other

24. Dietrich Bonhoeffer, *Life Together* (San Francisco: Harper One, 2009), 94.

25. Dan Allender, *The Wounded Heart: Hope for Adult Victims of Childhood Sexual Abuse* (Colorado Springs, CO: NavPress, 2008), 14.

26. Dietrich Bonhoeffer, *Life Together* (San Francisco: Harper One, 2009), 98.

27. Eric Metaxas, *Bonhoeffer: Pastor, Martyr, Prophet, Spy* (Nashville: Thomas Nelson, 2011), 69.

28. William White, *Stories For the Journey: A Sourcebook for Christian Storytellers*, (Minneapolis: Augsburg Publishing House, 1988), 48.

29. William Law, *A Serious Call to a Devout and Holy Life* (London: William Innys, 1729), available online at http://www.ccel.org/ccel/law/serious_call.txt.

Chapter 8: Live in Harmony with One Another

30. StringsMagazine.com. "Fellowship of the Strings, The Orpheus Chamber Orchestra Is Reinventing Group Dynamics." August 2012. http://www.allthingsstrings.com/News/Interviews-Profiles/Fellowship-of-the-Strings-the-Orpheus-Chamber-Orchestra-is-Reinventing-Group-Dynamics

31. Huffington Post. "Crews begin burning house teetering on Texas cliff." June 13, 2014. http://www.huffingtonpost.com/huff-wires/20140613/us--texas-house-cliff/

32. A. W. Tozer, *The Pursuit of God* (Charleston, SC: Create Space, 2013), 52.

33. C. S. Lewis, *Mere Christianity* (San Francisco: Harper One, 2015), 123.

Chapter 9: Speak the Truth in Love

34. National Academy of Sciences. "The NAS Building—the Einstein Memorial," 2016, http://www.nasonline.org/about-nas/visiting-nas/nas-building/the-einstein-memorial.html.

35. David Augsburger, *Caring Enough to Hear and Be Heard* (Harrisonburg, VA: Herald Press, 1982), 12.

Chapter 10: Members of His Household

36. C. S. Lewis, *The Weight of Glory* (San Francisco: Harper One, 2001), 18.

37. Max Lucado, *Traveling Light* (Nashville: Thomas Nelson, 2001), 157.

Note to the Reader

T he publisher invites you to share your response to the message of this book by writing Discovery House, P.O. Box 3566, Grand Rapids, MI 49501, USA. For information about other Discovery House books, music, or DVDs, contact us at the same address or call 1-800-653-8333. Find us online at dhp.org or send e-mail to books@dhp.org.